Spectacular Australian
SEA RESCUES

Spectacular Australian
SEA RESCUES

LIZ BYRSKI

Forewords by
Australian Maritime Safety Authority
and Isabelle Autissier

Published in Australia in 1997 by
New Holland Publishers Pty Ltd
3/2 Aquatic Drive
Frenchs Forest
NSW 2086 Australia

Cover design by Mark Seabrook
Typeset by Midland Typesetters
Printed in Australia by McPhersons Printing Group

National Library of Australia Cataloguing-in-Publication Data

Byrski, Liz.
Spectacular Australian sea rescues

ISBN 1 86436 301 0.

1. Search and rescue operations - Australia. 2. Shipwrecks -
Australia. 3. Survival after plane accidents, shipwrecks, etc. I. Title.

910.4520994

Cover Picture Credits
Top left and centre right: Guy Magowan (The *West Australian*)
Top right, centre left and bottom right: Kerry Berrington (*Sunday
    Times*, Perth)
Bottom left: Nicholas Wilson (The *Advertiser*, Adelaide)

**This book is dedicated to
Australians who risk their lives to
save others from the sea.**

Acknowledgements

I am grateful to many people for their assistance in the preparation of this book and would like to thank them for their willingness to provide information and contacts. Particular thanks are due to my friend and colleague Karen Buck for invaluable assistance with research.

For sharing their personal stories, I would like to thank:
Colin Ward, Lyn and Bryce Quarrie, Richard 'Sam' Samuels, Reg Brown, Chris Terjesen, Julian Martin, Kyle Bates, Peter Dabbs, Commander Terry Roach, and Roger Meadmore.

Special thanks also to:
Captain Richard Purkiss, Department of Transport, Maritime Division, Fremantle
Squadron Leader, David Jeffcoat, Department of Defence
Richard Elvin, Kailis France Fisheries
Vic Jeffries, Royal Australian Navy, HMAS Stirling
Chris Payne, Australian Maritime Safety Authority, Fremantle
Guy Leyland, West Australian Fishing Industries Council
Gary Foley, Bureau of Meteorology, Perth
Greg Turner, Queensland Department of Transport and Gold Coast Air Sea Rescue
Kristin Quayle, 'Where Are They Now', television series, Channel 7
David Gray, Australian Maritime Safety Authority, Canberra

LIZ BYRSKI
Fremantle, Western Australia
June 1997

Foreword

In the dying days of 1996 and the first few days of the new year, a drama unprecedented in the annals of Australian maritime history unfolded on the Southern Ocean—the successful rescue of solo yachtsmen Raphael Dinelli, Thierry Dubois and Tony Bullimore. The drama captured the imagination not just of Australia but the world, and strengthened Australia's already formidable search and rescue reputation.

The Southern Ocean rescues were but three of scores carried out each year around Australia's vast coastline by a gallant band of volunteers and professionals, who regularly put themselves at extreme risk to help those in life-threatening situations. These people are the unsung heroes, and receive few accolades. They are content just to be a part of maritime fraternity intent on helping others survive at sea. Much was made in the aftermath of the Southern Ocean rescues of the cost of the operations. That is negative and unworthy. It diminishes the physical, emotional and professional contribution made by those involved in rescues, for whom such events are always harrowing in the extreme.

What is also certain is that the Southern Ocean rescues are but the most recent, and that others will surely follow. In recent months, Australia's search and rescue preparedness has been bolstered by the formation of AusSAR—Australian Search and Rescue. The new organisation, based in Canberra, brings together the coordination functions of the Australian Maritime Safety Authority and Airservices Australia, which previously had been responsible for aviation search and rescue. With the formation of AusSAR comes a more unified, strategic focus on Australia's civil search and rescue operations, which are carried out over one-ninth of the earth's surface. It also reinforces the fact that, seven days a week and around the clock, those in peril, not only on the sea but also over land, are in experienced and proven hands.

This book, a selection of Australia's most memorable rescue stories, has captured the essence of search and rescue in this country, and the key role played by those whose duty it has been to coordinate and carry out rescue missions over the years. It also reinforces a message rescuers have been invoking for years, and will no doubt continue to invoke—that nature is a fearsome, sometimes merciless foe, against whom every precaution needs to be taken.

We commend this book and congratulate those responsible for its publication.

AUSTRALIAN MARITIME SAFETY AUTHORITY
Canberra
July 1997

Foreword

I remember that December day, the sea was fuming with anger. Throughout the night the wind had been howling between 50 and 65 knots, my boat was speeding along, already under makeshift rigging. In this far-off austral/southern part of the world, at a latitude position of 50 degrees south, nature imposed its savagery and the world of humans was far, very far, away. By morning, the situation had gone beyhond hope of change. I remember hearing a sound like the thundering of a locomotive engine produced by a huge breaking wave — my universe turned upside down. The boat rolled over with the wave, then righted itself, ruined, mast broken, hatches ripped off, rudder blades torn apart, and full of water.

Prepared and trained as I was to manage any kind of crisis that a sole-navigator race around the world could give rise to, I rapidly made the diagnosis that this time, for the first time in my life, I was going to ask for help.

Humanity has paid such a heavy debt to the sea. Undoubtedly the sea has contributed much to us as a source of food, means of communication, discovery and adventure, but we will forever be outsiders in this watery environment, constantly obliged to struggle in order to survive it. How many dramas, known or unknown, how many lives lost, how much suffering?

But if humanity does not have the ease of seabirds or dolphins, we, alone among the species, have the magnificent quality of solidarity. This special quality of ours has often led to miracles in saving human lives, sometimes to the detriment of the rescuers themselves, who are carried off in their turn into the infernal spiral of the waves. On all the coasts of the world, magnificent and heroic pages have been written where others have risked everything in order to bring help.

At the beginning of this century, an international maritime agreement made provision that individual countries should be responsible for saving human life at sea free of charge, whatever the nationality of the sailors or the reason for their presence on the waters. This is so even for an enemy in time of war. How many landlubbers must envy this spirit of solidarity. Gradually countries have become equipped with trained, qualified personnel and resources to handle these functions, whether for an imprudent yacht or a super tanker in distress.

I have had the opportunity to experience the professionalism of these women and men, their skill in operating in the terrifying conditions of an angry austral/southern ocean, the intelligence of their thinking to maximise the success of the mission. I have also seen the pride on their faces and their joy when, after three days of struggle, I set foot on the bridge of the frigate Darwin.

We must thank these heroes for carrying out the finest profession in the world and for doing it with sincerity, warmth and professionalism. They represent the finest accomplishment of the maritime tradition. We can be proud of them.

ISABELLE AUTISSIER
France
August 1997

Contents

Introduction

Alongside the upturned hull of the yacht a man's head appeared above the water. Spluttering for breath, he swam desperately towards the rescue boat. He was swimming for the life he thought he had lost, summoning every last bit of energy to grasp his second chance at life. Tony Bullimore had thought he would die in the upturned hull of *Global Exide Challenger*. For four days he was trapped inside the cavern of his capsized yacht in freezing temperatures, and he had almost given up hope. But on 9 January 1997, the world watched as the determined lone yachtsman swam out from under his boat into the arms of rescuers. He was alive!

A couple of hours earlier and just a short distance away, Thierry Dubois had been plucked by helicopter from a life raft dropped four days earlier by the crew of an RAAF Orion. Dubois had been marooned for hours on the hull of his capsized yacht *Pour Amnesty International*. And only a few days before that, after standing for 22 hours on his sinking yacht, the *Algimouss*, Raphael Dinelli had been rescued by another solo yachtsman, Pete Goss, who was directed to the location by Australian rescue services.

The Southern Ocean rescues of these three 1996/97 Vendee Globe solo round-the-world yacht race competitors focused the world's attention on Australia. The determination, endurance, courage and stamina of the rescued men were matched by the outstanding coordination, management, skill, professionalism and bravery of the Australian search and rescue teams. The rescues were a triumph of the human spirit and a testimony to what Tony Bullimore later called 'the inbuilt spirit of Australia'.

These dramatic rescues are stories of courage and heroism and, like the very best adventure stories, they have happy endings. But the Southern Ocean rescues were not the first dramatic sea rescues to take place in Australian waters. In fact, Australia has a proud history of sea rescues and, although they do not all involve the large number of people and state-of-the-art technology of the Dinelli, Bullimore, and Dubois rescues, they are all stories of courage, bravery, endurance and that 'inbuilt spirit of Australia'.

In a nation surrounded entirely by water and with a coastline of 36 000 kilometres, it is hardly surprising that Australian waters are often the stage for extraordinary real life drama. The Australian search and rescue services are responsible for rescue operations over roughly 47 million square kilometres, 11 per cent of the world's surface. From evacuating complete crews of tankers and oil rigs to helping families who have encountered trouble on their recreational boats, the men and women of the rescue services regularly put their own lives at risk to rescue fellow human beings from the sea.

The 1997 Southern Ocean rescues involved the combined skills of the Australian Defence Forces and were coordinated by the Australian Maritime Safety Authority (AMSA), a largely self-funded Commonwealth safety agency which has a charter for enhancing efficiency in the delivery of safety and other services to the Australian maritime industry. The AMSA's Rescue Coordination Centre (RCC) is based in Canberra and is responsible for merchant ships at sea, but also assists state authorities in maritime search and rescue when required. As a signatory to the International Safety of Life at Sea Convention (1974), and the International Search and Rescue Convention (1979), Australia is responsible for search and rescue over vast areas of the Indian, Pacific and Southern Oceans. Search and rescue arrangements are coordinated in a national plan involving state and federal agencies which include AMSA, the Department of Defence and the police.

State police forces have the prime responsibility for the coordination of search and rescue operations involving recreational and fishing boats. In each state the role of the Water Police is pivotal in the coordination and rescue of thousands of people from small boats. As some of the stories in this book illustrate the Water Police regularly find themselves in life-threatening situations, often working alongside dedicated and experienced volunteers of the Australian Volunteer Coast Guard Association. This association has more than 2500 regular volunteers and is the largest single volunteer marine rescue organisation in Australia and the Southern Hemisphere. In addition to the Australian Volunteer Coast Guard Association, there are many individual, local volunteer rescue groups in operation around Australia.

In earlier times, the passengers and crews of the steamers, traders, migrant ships and fishing boats wrecked off Australia's shores had only skilled seamanship, human courage and endurance to assist them. Today, however, there is a huge range of sophisticated technology which greatly assists in locating and rescuing people in conditions which, only a few years ago, would have been hopeless.

One such technological advancement is the development of satellite networks. Used in conjunction with distress beacons, computer facsimile machines, echo sounding equipment and sonar buoys, these satellite networks can help to accurately pinpoint the location of boats in trouble and provide immediate communications links between them and their rescuers. It is now mandatory for boats more than three kilometres off Australian shores to carry distress beacons and many smaller yachts now also use the Global Positioning Systems, a precise navigational system which uses American satellites.

But despite this technology, it is the dedication and courage of human beings which ultimately saves lives. It is the aircraft and helicopter crews which spot the marooned yacht, the bobbing raft or the tiny blob of a human head in the water. It is the sailors and seafarers, the police and the volunteers who go to each other's aid in tankers, frigates, fishing boats, yachts, sometimes even in tiny open boats, crashing through huge seas and treacherous storms as they do so, to reach stricken vessels. It is the helicopter and air-craft crews who risk the dangerous winds to fly at low levels to drop survival kits, winch survivors aboard and return them to safety.

It is, in the end 'the inbuilt spirit of Australia' which makes Australian sea rescues possible, and it is that spirit which is celebrated in this book.

An Unexpected Sea Adventure

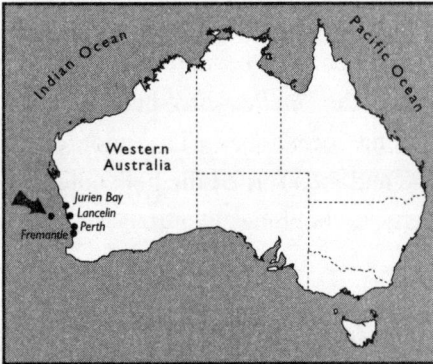

Rescue from the *Shelley Boy* off Green
Island, Western Australia, 14 February 1955.

*'Out there in the boats, it was wonderful to
see somebody close by.'* Skipper Robert Line.

The pilot had searched for the *Shelley Boy* and found it.
For almost five hours he had played a crucial role in
the rescue operation. He had directed the rescue vessels to
the boat and stayed above her, circling, watching, waiting.
In constant radio communication with the navy and other
boats he had been a vital cog in the intricate mechanics of
the rescue. The crew, and finally the skipper, had left the
boat and now she was tossing on the swell, pounded by
wind and driving rain.

Just the day before, the *Shelley Boy* had been a proud
and sturdy cray fishing and processing boat, a busy work-
place alive with the sound, smell and activity of the fishermen who worked on her. Now she lay empty and dying.

As the pilot watched, the boat rolled over on her side. She lay there for a minute or two, still and heavy in the surging water. It seemed almost as if she was taking her last breath. Then her stern began to sink and in 30 seconds it was all over. The *Shelley Boy* had disappeared, taking her secrets to the ocean bed. The pilot circled the area one more time and then turned the helicopter back to where the lifeboats were bobbing like toys on the waves 600 metres below.

The rescue of the skipper and crew of the *Shelley Boy* was one of the largest post-war rescue operations in Australian history. A dramatic incident off the west coast in 1955, it combined the efforts of the Royal Australian Navy (RAN) and the Royal Australian Air Force (RAAF) in a fast and spontaneous rescue operation which remains an example of the courage and efficiency of the defence forces working to save lives at sea.

The drama began on 14 February 1955. The attention of West Australians was captured by the annual Perth–Bunbury–Perth yacht race. As the last of the yachts were heading back to Fremantle, two RAN Corvette Minesweepers were standing by as attendants. HMAS *Junee* was situated off Rottnest Island and HMAS *Fremantle* was anchored off Fremantle port in Gage Roads.

Usually employed as training ships for national servicemen, the minesweepers' yacht race duties were almost at an end. On board with the crew were a number of journalists, some yacht race officials and an ABC radio announcer, all enjoying the last hours of the race. Suddenly, the atmosphere changed from the relaxed monitoring of the racing yachts to a tense and fast-paced struggle to rescue the crew of a sinking fishing boat.

The *Shelley Boy* was a wooden, diesel-powered vessel owned by Craypak Pty Ltd, a West Australian cray fishing and processing company. Built in Singapore only a couple of years earlier she was a sturdy 33-metre, 120-tonne craft designed for the tough job of cray fishing and processing. On 13 February she had been at sea for about 36 hours, her first trip since the completion of a 28-day overhaul and refit at Fremantle. It was Sunday evening and the crew was working as normal, some on work shifts and some resting. Most of them had no idea that water was leaking into the engine room—a slow but steady leak which would take a hold on the ship as the night wore on. Why and how the leak began is still shrouded in mystery, but all night the sea made its insidious way into the *Shelley Boy*.

At some point during the night the discovery of the leak was made and the crew immediately swung into action to save the boat. Pumps were used to get rid of the water, which by now had found its way into almost every part of the vessel. But the pumping was not enough and the skipper and crew were faced with the inevitable fact that their vessel was sinking.

At 6.45 a.m. on Monday, 14 February the skipper of *Shelley Boy*, Robert Line, radioed a distress signal to the mainland. He said the boat was taking water, there was already several feet of water in the engine room and he estimated that at some time between 11.00 a.m. and midday, the *Shelley Boy* would sink. Meanwhile, on board the crew worked on pumping and baling but their efforts seemed futile against the persistent flow of water pouring into the boat. Despite the hopelessness of the task, the crew struggled on, each man playing his part in the battle to save the *Shelley Boy*. As they worked, each confronted the prospect of, at worst going down with the boat and, at best a rescue which would bring its own untold dangers.

The distress call was picked up and relayed to HMAS *Leeuwin* in Fremantle, which immediately took over the coordination of the rescue. The navy was put on immediate alert and the HMAS *Junee* was on her way from Rottnest to the sinking boat by 7.30 a.m. HMAS *Fremantle* left her position in Gage Roads a little later, around 9.00 a.m. The Corvettes had no time to return to land before heading out of the Fremantle waters and up the coast, so for the civilians still on board it was an unexpected adventure.

The weather was unusually bad for the time of year. For the previous 24 hours, widespread rain and storms had covered most of Western Australia and the waters off its coast. More storms were forecast. A cyclone was located about 240 kilometres north-north-west of Carnarvon, further up the coast. Many of the state's airstrips were closed and ships at sea were reporting 30-knot winds.

The skippers of *Junee* and *Fremantle* estimated they would reach the distressed *Shelley Boy* at about 3.00 p.m. They knew that it would almost certainly be too late to save the boat, but there was still a good chance for the 17 seamen on board. The crews of the two Corvettes were pushing their vessels to the limits in order to reach the cray boat as fast as possible.

The navy had contacted the RAAF at Pearce Air Base,

about 35 kilometres from the West Australian coast. By 9.15 a.m. Wing Commander Saunders was airborne in the Dakota and searching for the *Shelley Boy*. Close behind the Dakota was a civilian Dove aircraft chartered by West Australian Newspapers with two journalists on board.

Saunders headed straight to the reported position of the *Shelley Boy*, but as he flew out over the sea the weather conditions worsened, bringing visibility down to a minimum. The heavy rain and cloud made the search frustrating, as well as hazardous.

Focusing intently on the surging surface of the ocean, the crew of the Dakota combed the designated area looking for glimpses of a vessel through the swirling clouds and heavy rain. It was almost 11.00 a.m. when Saunders was able to radio back to rescue coordinators that he had sighted the distressed boat, 18 nautical miles west of her originally reported position. It had taken them almost two hours to locate her. Saunders was determined to keep the cray boat in his view and continued circling above her. She was still afloat but time was racing along. If Robert Line's prediction was correct, she could go down at any time. It was crucial that when the time came to abandon ship, the Dakota still had the *Shelley Boy* in its sights.

When they heard the sound of the Dakota's engines above, the crew of the *Shelley Boy* whooped and cheered with relief. Their efforts to keep up a pumping regime and make the boat as safe as possible had left them cold, wet and exhausted. They knew they had reached the limits of what they could do, very soon it would be too unsafe to stay on the boat. They began to think about taking their chances in the lifeboats; once there the wait for rescue could still be a long one in very dangerous seas.

Robert Line's early morning distress signal had also been picked up by some fellow fishing boats. The spirit of mateship is legendary among those who work the oceans and this time was no exception. Because of the weather, many of the fishing boats that would normally have been out at sea that day had stayed in port. But almost immediately, four cray boats responded to the call. From Lancelin, Cervantes and Green Island they came ploughing through the turbulent waters. The *John Jim, Villaret, Pacific Pride* and *Blue Finn* abandoned their work to see if they could help their mates. Relying on gut feeling, intuition and their years of experience at sea, they braved the huge swell and blinding rain. Monitoring the area from 600 metres above, Saunders observed this small but determined civilian flotilla on the mission to help rescue the crew of the *Shelley Boy*. Pushing on bravely, they bobbed like corks on the huge waves, taking water over the decks and becoming shrouded in rain and spray. The waters were a raging mass of white foam from the breaking waves, which were crossing each other and tumbling in all directions.

Despite this mighty struggle, the conditions proved too much for the cray boats. One by one, the skippers acknowledged that they were putting the safety of their own crews in danger and adding to the hazard of the rescue. They must abandon the search and get out of the area. To continue would be risking further disaster and the Corvettes would be rescuing the crews of more than just one cray boat from the ocean.

The *Shelley Boy* was having difficulty keeping in radio contact with the mainland but she was able to maintain constant contact with one of the cray fishing boats, the *John Jim*. So while the others made their way back to the shore, the skipper of the *John Jim* decided to stay in the general area to pass on messages between the *Shelley Boy* and the rescue teams, as well as provide moral support to the crew of the stricken boat.

Meanwhile on the *Shelley Boy*, the water level was rising at an alarming rate. By 11.30 a.m. the water in the engine room was two metres high. Robert Line knew that the time to abandon ship was fast arriving. Judging the timing of when to leave the boat was crucial. Getting into the lifeboats in these weather conditions was a huge risk in itself, and the longer he and his crew spent in the little lifeboats, the greater the chances were of the lifeboats being overturned or of crew being washed overboard into the heavy seas. It was still some time before they could expect the arrival of the Corvettes, so he wanted to keep the crew on board as long as it was safely possible.

Robert Line decided that the 16 crew members should be divided between the two available lifeboats—eight men in each. As for himself, he was determined to stay with the *Shelley Boy* until the last possible moment. He knew that the *Junee* and *Fremantle* were carrying portable diesel pumps. If they arrived in time it might be possible to pump out some of the water and salvage the boat. The Corvettes had given a revised, estimated arrival time of 1.30 p.m. Line wanted to stay with his boat until the Corvettes arrived, taking on the ropes and assisting with any possible salvage attempt.

Line radioed a message to Wing Commander Saunders in the Dakota, asking him to drop some lifebelts and inflatable rafts as the crew would soon abandon ship. The drop was crucial and demanded extremely skilled flying. The Dakota needed to be in a position where the flight crew could drop the equipment as close as possible to the *Shelley Boy*. Saunders successfully made the drop at 12.07 p.m. and Robert Line now had the equipment he needed to ensure maximum safety for his crew, and two extra life rafts which would allow him to stay on the boat after the crew disembarked.

A skipper's first responsibility is to his crew, and most of the men on the *Shelley Boy* were cray processors with only limited experience at sea. However, Robert Line was impressed by their discipline and good sense. They had done a valiant job of trying to save the boat and had remained calm. Now they had to handle the tricky job of launching the lifeboats and coping with the significance of abandoning the ship in huge seas.

The launch of the first boat went like clockwork, rising and hanging out in textbook fashion over the water and steadily lowering down until it was afloat. Line breathed a sigh of relief. With only their life jackets and the clothes they were wearing the first eight men went calmly but very quickly over the side of the now listing *Shelley Boy*. As the men slipped down the ropes and into the tiny exposed lifeboat, massive swells rocked the cray boat and dragged her further down.

Although tossing wildly in the lifeboat, the eight men waved up reassuringly to the remaining crew on the deck. There was a sense of safety in being in the lifeboat away from the pull of the rapidly sinking vessel. The waves began breaking over them and fierce winds were driving the heavy rain at them with uncomfortable force.

The launch of the first lifeboat had gone like a dream. Line gave the order to launch the second and this time the dream turned to nightmare. The *Shelley Boy* was listing so badly that the lifeboat was hanging over her deck instead of over the sea. She hung there perilously, swaying back and forth in the wind and the heavy rocking of the vessel. At any moment she could break loose and crash down onto the deck, the men could be killed and the *Shelley Boy* sunk within minutes.

Line knew they had to get the lifeboat clear of the side of the boat and into the water as quickly as possible. Every minute vastly increased the danger. He ordered the crew to disconnect the lifeboat davits. As they did so, they shot her out over the stern like a rocket. It was a heart-stopping moment for the men whose lives depended on getting the lifeboat off its perilous fixings, over the deck and safely into the water. She rocked wildly before settling on the swell. In the same swift and orderly way as the first eight men, the remaining crew members slipped over the side and into the second lifeboat. It had seemed like an eternity but the whole operation—from the order to abandon ship to the moment the last man entered the lifeboat—had taken only six minutes. Robert Line was now alone on his sinking boat.

Overhead in the Dakota, Saunders maintained his watch over the *Shelley Boy* and marvelled at the speed and efficiency of the operation. Meanwhile, his radio operator, Warrant Officer Edwards, in cooperation with the Dove aircraft, was directing the two Corvettes towards the scene.

They were still a good way off and doubts began to arise about the 1.30 p.m. arrival time. The original estimated time of 3.00 p.m. now seemed more likely.

Alone on the *Shelley Boy* Robert Line sadly surveyed his boat's condition, all the while staying in radio contact with the skipper of the *John Jim*. He was not yet ready to give up and was still hoping against hope that the navy would arrive in time to attempt a salvage operation.

Out on the water the men had roped the two lifeboats together with about 120 metres of heavy line to stop them drifting too far apart. With eight men in each, the boats were crowded and the crew knew that it could be two or three hours before they were picked up. They had lashed one of the inflatable rafts to one of the boats and two crew members clambered into the raft and the conditions were eased somewhat. Displaying the patience and discipline of the night before, they faced the long and dangerous wait ahead. The aircraft overhead was reassuring but it could not pluck them from the lifeboats which were tossing like matchboxes on the big waves.

Despite Robert Line's estimations, the *Shelley Boy* was still afloat at 12.30 p.m. As 1.00 p.m. came and went, the water continued flowing into the boat's hull. At 1.20 p.m. the Corvettes finally had sight of the boat and were heading towards her at 15 knots. But it would be at least half an hour before they arrived. By 1.40 p.m. Line knew it was time to go. He radioed his intention to abandon ship and sadly bade her farewell. He climbed into the remaining inflatable raft lashed to the side of the boat, cut her loose, and vigorously rowed away from the *Shelley Boy* towards the other lifeboats. Ten minutes later, the *Shelley Boy* took her last breath and sank to 500 fathoms. All that remained of her was a mass of debris floating on the surface of the water, and an oil slick, dark and heavy in the foam.

It was about 2.15 p.m. when the Dove sighted the Corvettes about two nautical miles from the area. Soon after, to their great relief, the crew of the *Shelley Boy* also spotted *Junee* and *Fremantle*, two grey blurs taking shape as they emerged through the heavy rain and spray. The weather had reduced visibility down to about five nautical miles and the wild seas still raged. Captain Nelson in the Dove twice flew out to the Corvettes to guide them directly to the area. Taking the Dove down to 150 metres, he circled the lifeboats where the survivors, in their vivid yellow life jackets, waved in appreciation. Great skill and seamanship were required to manoeuvre the large Corvettes into a position from where they could get the men aboard, but not destabilise or otherwise endanger the lifeboats.

Finally, with each Corvette carefully positioned for maximum safety, the crews of the *Junee* and *Fremantle* threw scrambling nets, lifesaving ladders and ropes over the side of the ships. Shaking with cold and exhaustion, the survivors of the *Shelley Boy* began the perilous climb up the side of the Corvettes. The crews attempted to keep the nets, ladders and ropes steady as the Corvettes rolled around in the rough seas, but it proved to be a long and difficult process.

One by one the survivors, shaking with exhaustion, scrambled to the safety of the Corvettes' decks, grasping the ropes with frozen hands and struggling to get a firm foothold as the wind howled and rain lashed them. Those waiting to make the ascent hung on for their lives as the little lifeboats rolled dangerously beside the large mine-sweepers. Finally, Robert Line, the last of the survivors, clambered up the side of the Corvette from his inflatable raft. The ordeal was finally over.

As the 17 survivors lay below in crew bunks, thick blankets and mugs of steaming hot tea and cocoa slowly revived them. As the warmth worked its way into their bodies they contemplated the last 24 hours. Most of them had abandoned the *Shelley Boy* with only the clothes on their backs. Other clothes and possessions, such as bedding, personal items, money and valuables, had all been lost along with the *Shelley Boy*. While some survivors had family and loved ones waiting for them on shore in Fremantle, for others, the *Shelley Boy* had been their home and they would have nowhere to go to when they reached port. The relief of their rescue and the comfort and safety of the naval boats was soon tempered by the sense of loss and a fear of the immediate future.

With the survivors safely on board, the naval crews set about recovering the *Shelley Boy*'s lifeboats, an operation which took about 30 minutes. Then they were free to leave the area and the Corvettes radioed the mainland with the news that they were heading for Fremantle at a speed of nine knots. The Dakota and the Dove circled the area one last time before heading back to base. HMAS *Fremantle* and HMAS *Junee* arrived in Fremantle harbour almost 12 hours later in the dark and cold hours of the early morning. They were greeted by relieved wives of some of the survivors and a contingent of local journalists and photographers.

It had been 20 hours since the *Shelley Boy* had made its SOS call, 20 hours of terror in which the survivors had experienced every emotion from fear and desperation, to hope and relief. 'Without the RAAF Dakota we would not have had a chance, and when the navy arrived our troubles were over,' Skipper Robert Line told waiting reporters.

For the owners of the *Shelley Boy*, Craypak Pty Ltd, the loss was significant. The boat had been insured but it was the only process boat in the company's ten-vessel fleet. Even after reimbursement by the insurance company, it cost Craypak more than $80 000 in loss of equipment, stock and business.

For the crews of the RAAF and the RAN, the rescue from the *Shelley Boy* was a gruelling exercise carried out with great speed and efficiency, giving the national servicemen on board the two Corvettes another dimension to the experience of life in the defence forces. For the crew of the *Shelley Boy*, it was a brush with death that none of them would ever forget, and a voyage of self-discovery none had expected as they set out that morning on what they thought would be just another ordinary cray fishing run. For those who had lost everything on the *Shelley Boy*, clothing and accommodation had been provided within a few hours of their arrival in Fremantle.

Due to the skilled flying and search techniques of the RAAF and the prompt action and outstanding seamanship of the captains and crews of HMAS *Junee* and HMAS *Fremantle*, 17 lives had been saved in what remains one of the largest post-war rescue operations off the coast of Western Australia.

A Loss of Twenty-One Lives

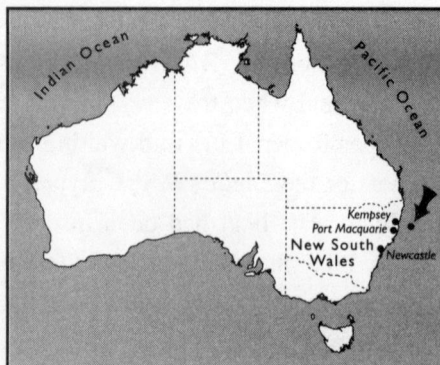

The sinking of the *Noongah* off Kempsey,
New South Wales, 25 August 1969.

*'I was standing at the stern. She went
straight down . . . straight under.'* Assistant
steward Anwyl Durose.

In the dark and stormy waters surrounding the sinking
freighter, men were floundering in huge waves. The tiny
red lights on their life jackets rose and fell along with the
swell, as their cries for help were carried away by the wind.
Some were struggling frantically to untangle themselves
from the ropes. Others were being swept away in the fierce
current and were grasping at bits of floating debris, desperate to find something which might act as a raft. On board
the ship, the captain was shouting to the remaining crew to
launch the lifeboats. Seconds after the ring of his final
command faded into the darkness, the *Noongah* sank below
the water.

Forty-eight hours later, pale and strained as they faced the crowd of reporters at a press conference, the survivors told their story of the sinking of the *Noongah* and their rescue from the mountainous seas. 'You can relax now,' a reporter suggested. 'It's all over.' John Wirth, second engineer on the vessel, shook his head. 'No it's not ... not for me. It will never be over. I've got to live with it. I keep thinking about it.'

When the 1493-tonne freighter *Noongah* came to grief off the north coast of New South Wales that dark and stormy night in August 1969, it became one of the great unsolved mysteries in modern shipping history. Built in 1955 at Port Glasgow, Scotland and owned by the Australian National Line (ANL), the *Noongah* was a heavy, slow ship—in fair weather she could only travel at a top speed of 10 knots. She also seemed to be an ill-fated ship. In May 1968, she lost most of her cargo in heavy seas in the Bass Strait. Five years earlier she had run aground after veering across the Brisbane River and striking a nine-metre launch.

On Monday, 25 August 1969, the *Noongah* was carrying 1499 tonnes of steel from Newcastle to Townsville. The cargo was loaded in her two holds and she had left Newcastle on Saturday afternoon with a crew of 26. For some of the crew it was their first voyage. The 35-year-old captain, Leo Botsman, had been at sea with ANL since the age of 19 and, although he had been master of the *Noongah* for only five weeks, he was very familiar with the ship, having served as her chief officer under the previous captain.

It had been a fairly uneventful run up the east coast until Sunday night, when the freighter was 12 nautical miles north-east of Smokey Cape. At this point she moved into the scope of a small cyclonic depression which was centred south-east of Lismore. Captain Botsman soon found his ship tossing wildly in the rough seas. Winds gusting at 30 and 40 knots whipped the *Noongah* about as she valiantly pushed on through the waves and battled the weather throughout the night. It remains a mystery why, at around midnight, the ship started taking water in the first hold and she soon developed a severe list to starboard.

The *Noongah* was rapidly taking on water. With breath-taking speed, the situation developed from a sticky run through a storm to a total disaster. By 3.45 a.m. the freigh-ter's engines were overheating and had to be stopped. The dangerous 12-degree list could not be corrected and Captain Botsman broadcast a radio distress call announcing the ship's predicament. He gave the *Noongah*'s position as 12 nautical miles off Kempsey, and appealed to other boats in the area to come to their aid.

Although no one was sure what was happening, there was little panic on board. Galvanised by the severity of the situation, each man went about his duty with an air of calm efficiency. Regardless of what they were feeling individu-ally about the situation, the crew was working as a unit to keep the ship afloat.

John Lingard, a 51-year-old greaser, had spent most of his life at sea and was no stranger to emergencies. The pre-vious year he had been on board the *Noongah*'s sister ship, the *Nilpena*, which had rolled over in the Bass Strait. The *Nilpena* crew had used saws and axes to cut away the timber on the cargo deck and the boat had righted herself. Lingard was optimistic that the *Noongah*'s situation that night would also right itself. As the boat started to take on water, the main lighting had failed. In the semi-darkness of the engine room second engineer, John Wirth, was working fast to activate the ship's emergency lighting.

The winds continued to howl around the ship and waves broke over the deck, gushing down the steep slope as she leaned down to the surface of the water. Anwyl Durose, an assistant steward, saw the water rising in the ship. He had been at sea only a month, but as he heard the ship's whistle, he recognised it as the signal to stand by to abandon ship. A chill ran down his spine as he tried to maintain his calm.

Down in the engine room John Wirth, John Lingard and Russell Henderson were working hard to right the *Noongah*. Perhaps they were concentrating so hard, or perhaps the noise in the engine room muffled the sound. For whatever reason, they did not hear the ship's whistle.

Within minutes of Captain Botsman sending his distress call, several ships altered their course to head for the *Noongah*'s location. The bulk carrier *Lake Boga* was the nearest vessel at a distance of about 30 nautical miles. Her skipper immediately changed direction and went in search of the stricken freighter. But the gale force winds and heavy seas made the journey arduous and slow and she could only progress at eight knots.

The Regional Director of the Department of Shipping and Transport was asleep at his home in Pymble, North Sydney, when the distress call was picked up on the radio. Within 20 minutes of receiving the telephone call bearing the news, Captain Taylor was up and on his way to his office in Sydney Cove to take over the coordination of the search and rescue operation.

RAN Destroyers HMAS *Hobart* and HMAS *Vendetta* were employed on exercises off Sydney, but 20 minutes after they were informed of the *Noongah*'s distress call, they diverted north to join the search. The RAAF dispatched a Hercules C130 from Richmond Air Base, north-west of Sydney, to the disaster site in order to assess the situation from the air.

The radio operators of the search and rescue team also managed to make contact with the Japanese tanker *Koyo Maru* and the freighter *Meringa*, who were both within accessible distance of the *Noongah*, and made haste to assist her.

On board the sinking ship, the crew could scarcely believe what was happening. It seemed only minutes since they had been making headway on course through the storm. Now their ship was sinking rapidly beneath them and some crew were donning life jackets. The situation on the deck was fast becoming chaotic. About 40 minutes after giving the standby signal, Captain Botsman knew it was time to give the order to abandon ship.

The *Noongah* had two lifeboats, each capable of carrying 32 men. Able Seaman, William Cockley with other crew members, was attempting to free the lifeboats from their fixings. As they struggled with the ropes, the rain lashed them, making it hard to see. The beating rain and the raging ocean were drowning out attempts at communication. As they dragged the covers off the lifeboat and set about trying to launch it, they soon realised that the ship's list was too great for either of the boats to be put to sea. They would have to jump overboard.

As the master ordered the whistle to be blown, indicating the final order to abandon ship, the last few men hurriedly grabbed life jackets and put them on. At 4.40 a.m. Captain Botsman sent his final radio message, briefly stating the crew's intention to abandon ship and that he was closing down the radio. He did not mention the problem with the lifeboats before the connection was cut, and from that point onwards, radio operators could not make any contact with the *Noongah*.

On deck, each man was choosing his own moment to take the terrifying leap over the side of the boat and into the life-threatening waters. Some stood frozen in terror. Others leapt desperately over the side, frantic to get as far away as possible from the vessel before she began her final drag down to the ocean bed. One or two stopped to grasp a mate by the hand before going overboard, while others paused to offer up a final prayer.

The wind was still gusting furiously, ripping and buffeting the men as they went over the side. Great waves were breaking over the bow of the ship, which by now was lifting sharply out of the water as the stern sank lower. The noise of the storm was interlaced with the yells and cries of the men who were trying to locate each other, and gave voice to their terror as the dark and cavernous ocean beckoned.

John Wirth struggled blindly out of the engine room and up against the sharp angle of the ship, making his way to the stern. John Lingard and Russell Henderson had battled their way out some minutes earlier and were already at the stern, frantically struggling into their orange life jackets.

Lingard saw Captain Leo Botsman on the steps leading down from the bridge. The master was yelling out to the men, urging them off the ship. Botsman remained on the steps as he watched his crew leave the *Noongah* to take their chances in the water. A lone figure silhouetted against the last remaining section of the ship above the water, the captain stayed on board, making no attempt to save himself. Seconds later, Lingard and Henderson were swept down off the stern and into the depths of the water.

Anwyl Durose, the assistant steward, knew these were the final moments. Wearing his life jacket, he was at the point of summoning his courage to jump when the boat shifted downwards and he was pulled under in the tug of her great bulk. As the *Noongah* finally disappeared under the waves, Durose felt the powerful force of the ship dragging him down. He fought wildly, his legs and arms flailing as he struggled against the railings, ropes and bits of plank which entrapped him. His lungs were bursting and the frantic fight for life back up to the surface seemed endless. Finally, his head broke the water and he gulped thankfully and gasped for breath.

In the rain and darkness, Durose was tossed around by the huge seas. It was almost impossible to see but he could hear the voices of the other men crying out, cursing and screaming in fear and panic. Some way off he spotted a dim light in the water. Durose swam towards it, fighting the waves that swamped him and left him gasping for breath. As he got closer he could see that the light was coming from one of the *Noongah*'s life rafts. Spurred on by his good fortune, he reached the life raft. It was already half full of water but he hauled himself over its side. Now that he was on the surface of the water, he could see the light shining from the lighthouse on the coast. He searched for the raft's paddle and, mustering all his strength, paddled to turn the raft so that its back was facing the sea. Durose knew that unless he kept the life raft's back to the waves, the small and already unstable raft would immediately capsize.

After being swept off the stern of the *Noongah* and into the sea, John Lingard fought his way back to the surface. As the confused current and the pull of the sunken ship dragged him in all directions, he could see pinpoint flashing coming from the lights of his shipmates' life jackets and could hear their frantic and panic-stricken cries. In the darkness and driving rain, he thrashed about in the water looking for anything which would help him to stay afloat. Although he was wearing a life jacket it was not providing enough support for his body to stay high enough in the water. As the waves washed over his head, he wondered how long he would be there and whether he would die in this dark, wild ocean. He had been at sea all his life and now it seemed he would end his life there too.

Through the rain Lingard caught sight of what he thought was a floating plank and he thrashed his way towards it. The plank turned out to be a large painter's platform, the sort used to hang over the side of a ship when in dock. Lingard dragged himself onto the floating platform and was soon joined by third engineer Russell Henderson, Able Seaman William Cockley, and the chief cook, Tom Ford, a man in his late sixties.

From the water the cries of their comrades echoed into the darkness. It was impossible for the four men to control, let alone steer, the platform. Caught on a raging current, it was swept along wherever the water chose to take it. As the six-metre-high waves hurled the platform up and down, Tom Ford was swept off and quickly lost in the swell. In the darkness and churning waters the others had no hope of finding him. Lingard, Henderson and Cockley decided to use the ropes hanging off the platform to tie themselves together. They figured they had a better chance of survival if they stayed together. If they were tipped off the platform they could also provide each other with extra buoyancy.

John Wirth had not been able to find a life jacket. Just before the *Noongah* went down he jumped from the stern into the water. Like the others, he surfaced to the blinding chaos of the raging sea and furious winds. For some time he floated hopelessly. Without a life jacket he knew his chances of survival were minimal. But he soon fell upon an extraordinary stroke of luck. In the dark he felt something bump against him. It was a life jacket! As he struggled in the water, he managed to drag it over his head.

Some time later, Wirth caught sight of the *Noongah*'s second life raft. He swam to it and dragged himself into its comparative safety. Frightened, shocked and exhausted, Wirth sprawled out in the raft and acknowledged his extraordinary luck. Still far from safety, he prepared himself for a long and lonely vigil on the cold, turbulent seas. As the force of the storm threw the raft around and the waves crashed over it, Wirth wondered about his shipmates. Had the others reached safety? Had they been dragged down with the ship? Or were there still men in the sea, floating in their life jackets, frozen and terrified, wondering if each wave was the last?

At 7.30 a.m. at her home in the Melbourne suburb of Glen Waverley, Pamela Botsman, wife of the *Noongah*'s master, received a telephone call from her mother-in-law. Mrs Botsman senior had heard of the *Noongah*'s distress call on the radio news. Numb with anxiety, Pamela Botsman tried to find out more but had to wait until the ANL offices opened at 9.15 a.m. to get further information.

The bad news of the freighter was rapidly beginning to spread that Monday morning in August 1969. In the homes of the 26 *Noongah* crew, fear and anxiety were growing as relatives waited for the latest fragments of information which might tell them the fate of their husbands, lovers, fathers, brothers and sons.

It was 8.20 a.m. by the time the *Lake Boga* fought her way through the storm to reach the *Noongah*'s last known location. Upon its arrival no trace could be found of the ship or any survivors. The spot was marked only by some debris and a faint oil slick. The search and rescue team were unaware that the *Noongah*'s lifeboats had not been launched and were expecting to find the crew safely in the boats. As well as HMAS *Hobart* and HMAS *Vendetta*, a third Destroyer, HMAS *Anzac* had joined the search, along with RAN Destroyer escorts *Derwent* and *Yarra*, and three Mine-sweepers *Hawk, Gull* and *Curlew*.

The Hercules aircraft that had been dispatched from Richmond Air Base during the night was busy searching the area. Pilot Flight Lieutenant Robson had spent an hour and a half tracing his way around the area. The flight crew were straining their eyes for signs of lifeboats, tiny specks of orange which might be a life jacket, or dark blobs which could turn into the head and shoulders of men in the swirling white water below. At about 8.45 a.m. their navigator Flight Lieutenant Williams spotted a distress flare marking not a lifeboat, but a raft tossing on the waves.

The raft was about 20 nautical miles south-west of the *Noongah*'s last recorded position and Robson marked the spot with a two-hour smoke flare then flew out to sea towards the *Koyo Maru* to guide the Japanese ship towards the raft. About a mile and half further on, Williams spotted another raft and the aircraft crew could see a man hanging on inside it. Robson circled the raft and dropped another smoke flare to mark its spot.

John Wirth had no idea how long he had been in the raft. He was still dazed by the last awful minutes of the *Noongah*'s sinking and his frantic struggle to survive in the ocean. Stunned and terrified, he huddled on the raft hoping and praying for his life. The sudden sight of the Hercules seemed the answer to his prayers and he rightly guessed that within a short time rescue would arrive.

Guided by the Hercules aircraft, Captain Kawakita of the *Koyo Maru* steered his ship through the last few miles towards Wirth's raft. He had to get close enough to the raft to be able to throw a line to the survivor, but not so close that the tiny raft would be dragged in the freighter's wake, dangerously close to its hull.

John Wirth, believing himself to be the luckiest man in the world, grabbed hold of the lifeline and pulled on it, hauling his raft closer to the Japanese freighter until he was close enough to kick free of the raft. Then he climbed up the lifeline until the arms of the *Koyo Maru*'s crew could stretch down and haul him up the last few metres to the safety of the deck.

The crew in the Hercules breathed a sigh of relief. At least one survivor was now safe on board. Now it was time to turn their attention to the second life raft nearby. Unfortunately, language difficulties had caused a misunderstanding and the *Koyo Maru* had changed direction and was moving away from the area of the life raft. Flight Lieutenant Robson quickly flew in the direction of the ship and circled it, signalling to it to follow the aircraft. This time, Captain Kawakita understood the signal and changing course again, followed the Hercules to where the other life raft was rolling perilously on the high waves.

In his waterlogged raft, Anwyl Durose welcomed the sight of the bulky ship heading towards him. Above him was the comforting presence of the circling Hercules. The *Koyo Maru* drew nearer until she was close enough for Durose to grasp the lifeline and drag himself in closer to the ship and then out of the raft. The crew of the *Koyo Maru* pulled him the last few metres onto the deck and there he discovered that one of his shipmates had also made it to safety.

Anwyl Durose and John Wirth had been in and on the water for almost five hours. They were cold, exhausted and deeply shocked by the terrifying events of the previous night. The Japanese crew brought them warm food and blankets and they were further comforted with the promise of a fast course to Brisbane and the prospect of being reunited with their wives and children. As the *Koyo Maru* set course for Brisbane the two men wondered anxiously what had happened to their colleagues and whether they were the *Noongah*'s only survivors.

As the morning wore on, the ships involved in the search and rescue party continued combing the area for more survivors. Early in the afternoon a media chartered twin-engine aircraft carrying journalists from the *Sydney Morning Herald* and Channel 7, joined the search. Flying as low as they could over the search area, they scanned the surface of the water. The sea was still pounding relentlessly. The high breaking waves were causing a heavy spray and this, combined with the driving rain, was making visibility very difficult. As the aircraft combed the area the crew thought they spotted a life raft. The pilot, George Rickie, brought the plane down to around 30 metres and it soon became apparent that the raft was in fact a wooden platform about four metres long and a metre and a half wide. On the platform, three men in orange life jackets were waving frantically. They were tied together in a line. At the end of the line was the body of a fourth man. As the aircraft circled the platform, the reporters could see the relief on the faces of the men below. George Rickie radioed the news to the search and rescue control centre at Coffs Harbour.

Lingard, Henderson and Cockley had been drifting uncontrollably on their perilous platform for more than 11 hours. Every pounding wave had brought with it the promise of disaster. As the hours wore on with no help in sight, their spirits had sunk. Their bodies ached with the effort of staying on the raft, and the wind and rain had chilled them to the bone. The body of a comrade floated by in the water. As they reached out to it and tied the body as best they could to the end of the platform, the true horror of their situation was brought home to them.

On a number of occasions they had seen vessels searching the area, but the rain and spray had hidden them from the sight of the searchers. Frantically they had waved and yelled, but knew that their efforts were useless in the blinding weather and howling storm. They had almost given up hope of being rescued.

When the three men saw the small plane overhead, a rush of hope and energy surged through them. They waved furiously and as it became clear that they had at last been seen, they shouted with relief. Help was finally on its way. It had been too late for their unfortunate mate but, thankfully, not for them.

The freighter *Meringa* was engaged in the search a couple of nautical miles further out to sea. When Coffs Harbour radio control received word of the sighting, it alerted the skipper of the *Meringa* to change course and head for the men's position. The search and rescue control centre then radioed George Rickie and requested him to fly over the platform and wobble the aircraft wings before flying in a straight line back over the bow of the *Meringa*. Watching the small aircraft complete its manoeuvre, the skipper of the *Meringa* was able to get an exact bearing on the survivors.

It took just 40 minutes for the freighter to reach the makeshift raft and move to a safe position alongside. The crew threw out lifelines to the survivors and the three men slipped off the platform and into the water. Grasping the lifelines, they were swept alongside the ship, dangerously close to the propellers. Swimming furiously away from the danger area, the men headed for the bow where the crew of the *Meringa* hauled them towards the rope ladders hanging over the side of the ship. Weak with cold and fatigue, the three men struggled up the rope ladders. A rousing welcome greeted them as they finally reached the helping hands of the *Meringa* crew.

Henderson, Lingard and Cockley were exhausted, albeit extremely relieved. They were grateful for their safety but were consumed with concern and anxiety for their shipmates. As they drank hot tea and rested comfortably on the *Meringa* they thought of their comrades still out there somewhere in the stormy ocean.

With 20 *Noongah* crew members still unaccounted for, the search continued. The body of the man who had been tied to the platform was later taken on board HMAS *Hobart*. Newspaper reports at the time did not identify him. The small media chartered plane later saw another body floating in the water but no more survivors.

By the time night fell there was no more news to raise the hopes of the many families waiting for word of their loved ones. Pamela Botsman had spent the whole day waiting for news of her husband, the captain of the *Noongah*. As the minutes ticked by, her heart grew heavier. Each time she heard the telephone ring she jumped out of her skin with a mixture of excitement and dread. She had tried to keep busy with her two-year-old daughter, and two-month-old baby son, but as the light of the day faded so too did her hopes.

Joy and Colin Pedemont waited in their Ashfield home in Sydney for news of their son, Stephen. The year before, Stephen had completed his radio operator's course and set his sights on going to sea. Just five days earlier he had been offered a job on the *Noongah* and had signed on for three months. It was Stephen's first voyage and, as they waited for news, the Pedemonts pictured their son alone in the huge waves and strong winds. They knew that Stephen's survival would be nothing less than a miracle.

For the families of the other missing *Noongah* crew it was an agonising time. As they counted the minutes and hours, they longed for the telephone call informing them that a miracle had occurred and their loved ones were safe. But it was not to be. There was no miracle for the Pedemonts or the families of the 21 other missing crew members.

On Tuesday, the day after the ship sank, three life jackets were found on Flynn Beach near Port Macquarie. The jackets were sodden and damaged, but had been carefully tied. On one of the jackets, the plastic whistle appeared to have been chewed, perhaps an indication of the terror its wearer was feeling at the time. It seemed that the life jackets had been dragged off the men by the force of the waves. Two more life jackets were later picked up by searchers near Kempsey.

The search for the *Noongah* survivors continued until Thursday. It was the largest land and sea search off the Australian coast and involved 15 commercial, private and RAN vessels as well as RAN and RAAF aircraft. Police combed the beaches, searching the coastline for washed-up bodies, and hundreds of volunteers turned out, training their

telescopes and binoculars for hours on the sea in the hope
that they would catch sight of one of the missing men. But
despite the huge effort, no more survivors were found.

The fact that five men had made it to safety was largely
due to the efforts of their rescuers; the skill of the RAAF
and civilian aircraft in spotting them and the outstanding
seamanship of the skippers and crew of the *Koyo Maru* and
Meringa, who manoeuvred their vessels so skilfully.

When Lingard, Wirth, Durose, Henderson and Cockley
finally faced reporters and told their story, they were devastated to find that none of their colleagues had survived
the terrible night in the ocean. John Wirth and Anwyl
Durose vowed they would never go to sea again.

The week following the rescue, the Minister for Shipping
and Transport ordered a departmental inquiry into the cause
of the disaster. This in turn led to the establishment of a
Court of Marine Inquiry. After an extensive investigation in
which the Court took evidence from survivors, their families, the ANL shipping company, the seamen's union and
many other interested parties, the Court handed down its
decision on 16 February 1970. The Court found that an
ingress of water to the first hold of the *Noongah* caused the
vessel to founder. The cause of that ingress could not be
determined from the evidence.

The *Noongah* was the first ANL ship ever to sink, taking
her secrets with her to the seabed, along with 21 lives.

Six Days in a Life Raft

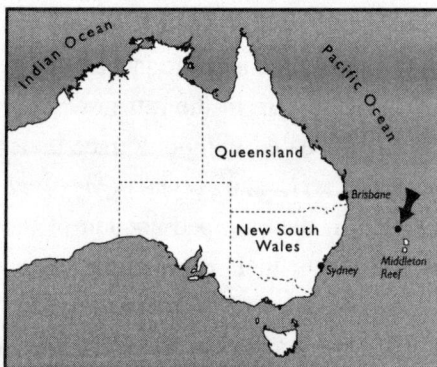

Rescue of the crew from the *One and All* off
Middleton Reef, Queensland, 8 October 1971.

*'We have had a talk. The RAAF must have
abandoned the search.'* Day 5 of the life
raft's log book.

Margaret Collins was determined to make it to the raft.
When she went over the side of the ketch she had
grabbed the log line instead of the paynter, and the raft had
drifted away. Behind her, the *One and All* was sinking, her
great bulk sliding silently beneath the waves.

Collins swam desperately. She tried to save energy by
surfing down the waves, her life jacket supporting her but
also restricting her movements. She had been in the water
for more than half an hour, fighting to narrow the gap
between herself and the raft. She knew the others were
trying to get back to her but they were downwind and the
breaking waves were confusing the swell. As she managed

to close in a little, John Baird leapt over the side of the inflatable life raft and helped her struggle the last few metres. As they reached the edge of the life raft the others grabbed hold of their arms and life jackets and hauled them aboard. They were all safe in the raft now, and their beautiful ketch had disappeared without a trace under the water.

Uncomfortably wet, the seven *One and All* crew members huddled in the cramped cocoon of the raft. They wondered where to put their legs amidst the cumbersome, hard-edged supplies they had thrown in from the boat at the last minute. They were safe, but this was just day one.

The *One and All* was a beautiful 101-year-old Tasmanian coastal trader. Made from 76 tonnes of Huon pine and spotted gum, she was filled with memories from the generations of seafarers who had loved her and sailed in her. In her original rig of gaff headed sails and top sails she would have been magnificent. But she was no relic. Despite her age, she was still a good, sound boat—sturdy and stable—and had captured the hearts and the imaginations of her current skipper and crew.

Peter Dabbs had bought the *One and All* in 1970 for $10 000. A photographer, journalist and filmmaker, Dabbs was an experienced sailor. The year before, a photoshoot had taken him to the Middleton and Elizabeth reefs, about 480 kilometres south-east of Brisbane, and the place had captured his imagination. He fell in love with the reefs and was determined to go back.

In 1971, Dabbs took on a contract to erect a non-directional radio beacon and light on the wreck of the *Runic*, a 13 858-tonne freighter of the Shaw Savill Line, which had foundered on the reef ten years earlier. Dabbs began to recruit people for the voyage and by the time the boat was ready to sail in October, he had assembled a motley crew. Jack Kenny was the only experienced seafarer among them. He had spent 23 years at sea and was a cautious and canny sailor. Ronald McIntosh was 29 and had served as an army artillery spotter in Vietnam. He was now working as a spray-painter and was looking for an exciting way to spend his annual leave. Twenty-six-year-old John Baird was, like Skipper Peter Dabbs, a film producer. He had just come back from a trip to England and with no work around, decided the trip would be a pleasant interlude.

The three other crew members were younger. Gary Deacon, 20, was the diver. He had worked before on trawlers in Australia and overseas, and had dreams of being a lighthouse keeper. He spotted the *One and All* in Moreton Bay and fell in love with her. All that 18-year-old James Perrin knew about the sea, he had learned in the surf on the Sunshine Coast. He was an apprentice motor mechanic and he reorganised his holiday to sail with the *One and All*. Margaret Collins was the most controversial crew member. Twenty-one years old, she had dropped out of her arts degree studies at university to work. She had some previous sailing experience and had met up with Dabbs after a lecture he had given to the Adventurers' Club in Brisbane. Margaret fell in love with the *One and All* and from the time she first saw the boat it never sailed again without her on board. In those days, the prospect of a young woman going to sea with six men caused a few raised eyebrows and arch comments. 'Can't anyone realise that seven people can go to sea, not as men and women, but as human beings?' she asked a reporter.

It was not only the beautiful old ketch that drew the crew together but also the lure of the reef and the glorious lagoon encircled by it. Middleton Reef was discovered in 1788 and lies close to the shipping routes from eastern Australia to Asia, the Pacific and the west coast of America. As well as a paradise for skin divers, this stretch of reef has proved to be a graveyard for sailors—at least 17 ships have been wrecked on it.

Aware of the reef's reputation, the crew left Brisbane in fine weather with the energy and enthusiasm of people setting out on an adventure. Dabbs reckoned it would take them about 50 hours of sailing to reach their target. It was daybreak when they came within sight of the reef. Jack Kenny and Ronald McIntosh were on watch and Kenny was about to take some sights with the sextant when they saw the reef ahead of them.

As the day broke, the weather changed bringing with it strong winds and rough seas with large cross waves. It was impossible to tell which surf was due to normal water breaking in the weather and which of it was surf breaking on the reef. The *One and All* circled the reef, trying to find a way in. The conditions became quite wild and huge seas developed. Dabbs was thrown from his bunk while Perrin was hurled almost three metres across the deckhouse.

Nevertheless, they persisted and the *One and All* eventually found its way safely into the heart of the reef. From here they could get easy access to the wreck of the *Runic*. It took the crew ten days to complete the job of installing the light and the beacon. In addition, they installed a morse key. If, in future any more ships foundered here, they hoped it would prove to be useful.

Jack Kenny was ill at ease on the reef. He had enough experience at sea to sense the perils of being in such a location. He knew how quickly conditions could change and cause disaster to strike. The way the waters were pounding and breaking over the *Runic* was putting him on edge. He and Perrin were particularly glad when the job was finished and they could plan their return journey.

On Friday, 1 October, the *One and All* sailed from Middleton Reef in moderate seas with a north-easterly force six to seven wind. Dabbs believed the *One and All* sailed best with a combination of sail and engine and they had rigged the stay sail and mizzen and had a well set jib. But there was rapid deterioration in the weather and increasingly strong winds. By Saturday morning the weather was much worse and the conditions looked set to last. The ketch began to pitch dramatically in the huge waves. Water was breaking over the bow and as the conditions grew wilder, the jib blew out. Now the boat was tossing up and down, rising and falling dramatically. Then she made her hardest yet slam down into the water and there was a deafening crack.

They were in a whirlpool of floating debris, tree trunks, and lengths of wood, as well as a floating jetty which must have broken away from the mainland. The *One and All* started taking water rapidly. Dabbs and Kenny were concerned but not overly worried. They thought the pumps would be able to cope with the water, which had by now risen to the level of the floorboards in the engine room.

As it was time for the 9.00 a.m. radio check, Dabbs and Kenny decided to send out a 'possible assistance needed' (PAN) signal. The rest of the crew remained calm and was determined to stay that way, despite the worsening situation. They cracked jokes and swapped witticisms, as much to reassure themselves as each other. It became harder, however, when they discovered that the waves breaking over the foredeck had submerged the pump and motor. The whole length of the *One and All*'s deck was now coming under crashing waves and the water level inside the boat was rising. However hard they worked they simply could not control the flow of water.

For over two hours they struggled to keep going. By about 11.20 a.m. Dabbs and Kenny acknowledged they were losing ground and broadcast a mayday call. Inside the boat it was chaos—everything was breaking loose from its bearings. The contents of the galley cupboards were flying around like missiles. The deep freeze, which had been bolted down to the deck and secured behind lengths of four-by-four timber, had been hurled out of its housing. Heavy with food, it crashed around, defying all attempts to secure it with cables.

The water inside the boat continued to rise and was coming in so fast that it was impossible to tell at what point or points it was actually entering the boat. As the ketch began to sink lower in the water, the waves breaking over her decks increased. Below deck, the flying freezer had ruptured a drum of diesel which was leaking fuel and noxious fumes. The crew knew that they would have to leave the *One and All* if they were to come out of this alive.

Despite the urgency and danger of their situation, abandoning the ketch was painful. For their own different reasons, the seven crew members had fallen in love with the *One and All*. With her graceful and dignified lines, her rich history and character, she was no ordinary boat. Although they had been aboard only a couple of weeks they had formed a special bond with her and through her, with each other.

The crew had maintained their sense of calm, swiftly and carefully doing all the things required before abandoning ship. They were in constant radio contact with Brisbane and Sydney and the operators reassuringly told Dabbs that a Neptune bomber on search and rescue could be expected to reach the area by about 3.30 p.m. It was now almost 2.00 p.m.

The formal language and almost laconic manner of the operator was in stark contrast to the chaos aboard the ketch. Peter Dabbs instructed the crew to go to the toilet and drink as much water as they possibly could, as their supply of fresh water would be limited. They needed to take food with them but most of it was stored in the dislodged freezer which was now inaccessible. They grabbed the food that had been stored in the cupboards, which by now was floating around in a mixed cocktail of seawater and diesel.

The boat was breaking up all around them, cracking, splitting, falling and crashing down. It was so noisy that it was almost impossible to hear the radio but they strained their ears to catch the calm, reassuring voice at the other end, telling them that everything would be all right. On deck, Peter Dabbs was holding the radio and Jack Kenny the battery. They were making the last call to Brisbane trying to hear and be heard above the roar of the wind and waves.

Earlier, the crew had donned life jackets. Now they threw the life raft over the side of the ketch and one of them pulled the cord which triggered the carbon dioxide cylinder attached to the bottom. The raft rapidly inflated, becoming a bright orange igloo bouncing on the big waves. At just over two metres in diameter, it was designed for only six people and was tiny. Hanging onto the rails, staggering, sliding and slipping on the now steeply sloping deck, they knew it was time to bale out. The ocean was pulling down on their boat. Water was pouring down the decks and they needed to be off the *One and All* with all speed.

As the others went over the side and into the raft, Jim Perrin suddenly changed direction. Hurling himself back against the wind and water, he switched on the boat's tape recorder. The guitar introduction to Simon and Garfunkel's *Sounds of Silence* rose up on the wind as Perrin struggled back and over the side into the raft.

'Hello darkness my old friend, I've come to talk with you again.' The haunting voices floated up, somehow audible on the wind above the turbulent sea. 'Because a vision softly creeping, left its seed while I was sleeping.' The ship sank a little lower, her sails full and drawing. 'And the vision that was planted in my brain still remains, within the sound of silence.' The stern of the ketch lifted high in the air and smoothly and silently she disappeared under the waves. It seemed as though she sailed down rather than sank. As the melody was muffled by the water, a small triangle of mizzen was the last fragment of the 101-year-old ketch to be seen. Only Jack Kenny had seen the *One and All* go down. The stillness and intensity of the moment had lasted only a second and Kenny was too preoccupied with the unfolding drama of Collins to reflect on its loss.

McIntosh, Deacon, Perrin and Baird had been the first to get into the life raft, and Collins was next. She had taken out her contact lenses and without them, mistook the paynter of the raft. She fell into the water and was rapidly being swept away. Dabbs and Kenny, still on the deck of the fast sinking *One and All*, immediately leapt onto the raft and they paddled furiously to try and reach her.

It took nearly 45 minutes before Margaret Collins was close enough for John Baird to go into the water and help her towards the raft. The others continued to paddle frantically to reach their foundering colleagues. At last Collins and Baird reached the edge of the raft. Tumbling, spluttering, breathless and exhausted, they were dragged aboard and into the tiny remaining space. The relief was immense.

The bond between the *One and All* crew was strong and somehow they all felt that as long as they stayed together and supported each other, they would survive this crisis. There had been no problems between them as they crewed and there would be no problems now. The conditions demanded absolute harmony and cooperation. The inside of the raft was only about one and a half metres across and they had to find a way of sitting which was comfortable enough for all of them. They lay in a circle, their backs against the edge and canopy of the raft and their feet in the middle. It was cramped and they hoped it wouldn't be too long before they were rescued. By now it was around 3.00 p.m. on Saturday, 2 October.

As the crew settled from the shock of leaving their boat, they began to investigate the contents of the emergency kit on board. There were food packs made up of concentrated food tablets and glucose tablets. These would supplement the meagre supplies they had managed to bring with them from the *One and All*. There were 23 tins of water, can openers, a measuring cup, a baling bucket, a torch with spare batteries, kits to stop leaks, spare valves, distress signals, parachute flares and a signalling mirror. The kit also contained six tubes of sea sickness pills. In 23 years at sea, Jack Kenny had never considered taking a sea sickness tablet, but with the raft lurching around, lunging up and down on the huge waves, he promptly swallowed one. For many of the others it was too late, and the baling bucket started to make its way around the circle. The sea sickness the crew suffered was a real worry. They knew it would dehydrate them and increase their need for the limited water supply.

There was also a survival guide on the raft indicating the calorific value of their food packs and how best to allocate the food and water between them. They would have to be very careful because the supplies were designed for six people, not seven. As they had left the boat, Peter Dabbs had ordered that only essentials should be taken into the raft, so he was surprised and somewhat annoyed to find that the hard lump under his backside was a jar of Brylcreem! No one would confess to its ownership, but the jar stayed on board.

The cold and wet crew members were soon stiff from

sitting in the cramped conditions. If one person moved, it automatically caused disruption to all the others. Clearly they would have to have some sort of system to allow them to move about a bit. They adopted the Arab bus passenger method: they all moved one way together and when someone felt cramped, they all moved together in the opposite direction. Leg cramps were a real problem and they tried a system of odd and even numbers, so that those allocated with odd numbers would stretch their legs out, while those who were even drew theirs up. Every ten minutes they would change. Then they tried taking it in turns for each person to have their legs on top of the other six pairs of legs for five minutes, and then change. Even so, there were times when one would have to move at a particular point as the discomfort of their legs became excruciating.

All through the night, hour after interminable hour, the sea pounded them relentlessly. The huge waves broke over the top of the raft canopy which kept collapsing onto their heads. They feared their necks would be broken by the terrifying weight and force of the water. But by the next morning weather conditions had improved.

Sunday dawned and they had seen no signs of a search aircraft. Jack Kenny put out the drogue so that they would not drift too far from the position which they had radioed to Brisbane. They talked about their situation and put some energy into housekeeping. They examined everything they had with them and figured how they could create more space in the cramped cocoon of the raft. There were able to rig up a makeshift hammock above their heads to hold things they weren't using, such as heavy sweaters. Other items were packed up, wrapped in a waterproof cover, attached to a rope and thrown in the water. The carefully rationed water was holding out well but those who were very seasick were allocated a little extra. The time dragged and began to wear them down. They all felt reasonably safe, the bond between them becoming a vitally important factor in their morale. They firmly believed they would be rescued. The question was when? The boredom and discomfort grew steadily.

On Monday afternoon they heard aircraft engines. At first only Margaret Collins could hear them. Minutes later, the rest of the crew could hear the steady throbbing in the distance. Although the crew couldn't see the planes or tell which direction they were coming from, they could hear them quite distinctly. They were clearly search aircraft because they seemed to make three passes each about 40 minutes apart.

The search and rescue expedition had been underway since Saturday afternoon, but weather conditions had been hampering the efforts of the RAAF Orions and Neptunes— the winds were strong and visibility was very poor. The aircraft had been moving back and forth relentlessly over the search area. The crews strained their eyes for the slightest speck which might possibly be survivors in the ocean, but they could see nothing.

On Sunday, the navy joined the search. With conditions too bad for many boats and others engaged in operations at a distance, HMAS *Otway*, an Oberon class submarine, was sent into service. At the time HMAS *Otway* was taking part in Navy Week activities in Brisbane. When the order came to sail, a number of crew had taken shore leave and Commander Terry Roach set out with only 43 of the usual 65 personnel. Roach had to rely on the versatility of his team to ensure that the submarine would run safely and efficiently, with some crew members undertaking tasks they had previously never performed.

Over the next few days, the search and rescue team combed a 6000-square-nautical-mile area around the Middleton Reef but they could find no sign of the survivors. By Tuesday morning, 5 October, there was talk of winding things up. When Australians opened their morning newspapers that day, the headlines informed them that two US Destroyers travelling from Brisbane to Auckland, the *Lang* and *Edison*, would join the search and make a sweep of the area. It seemed to be the last ditch attempt before giving up.

Meanwhile on the raft, the seven survivors could only speculate about the search. The previous day they had heard aircraft, but they had obviously not been sighted and they hadn't heard anything since. They discussed the possibility of trying to rig up a sail and attempting to sail to the coast. They established one hour shifts; one person would stay at the canopy opening of the life raft, watching and listening for any sight or sound of the rescuers. Each one tried to hang on to hope and to their nerves. They fidgeted about, shifting their legs and wondering how much longer it would be before help came, wondering if it would arrive before some other disaster overtook them.

Now that the weather had settled down it was fairly quiet in the raft. After the first wild night with its monstrous waves, the last two nights had been clear and calm. The moon was full, the skies clear and the waters still. The only disturbance was from barracuda leaping out of the water. The thrill of watching the fish was tempered by the fear that they might land on the raft and tear it. Peter Dabbs, half asleep, heard the hissing sound of air escaping and thought the raft was deflating. But it was just a rupture in one of the small air chambers at the base of the raft. The crew spent most of their time in a daze, half asleep, half awake. They didn't talk much. Dabbs had told the others at the outset that because they had little water, it was essential that they conserve their body moisture. Every time they opened their mouths they would lose moisture, so they should talk only when essential. But often they needed to talk about their families, their thoughts and their fears.

On Tuesday, the weather was still calm. The crew of *One and All* had been regularly monitoring their drift by throwing things overboard and timing their drift. Suddenly, during the late morning they heard aircraft engines again. At regular intervals the sounds came, and then late in the afternoon at about 4.15 p.m. they could actually see an aircraft far away in the distance. Their adrenalin began to flow. It looked as if the aircraft was coming their way. They fired a parachute flare, but the sun was behind them and the aircraft would have difficulty seeing it. Had they wasted a precious flare? They talked it through and agreed only to use flares again if it was absolutely certain the aircraft would be able to see them. They would use the signalling mirror and torch wherever possible.

A couple of hours later, they heard the sound of a jet aircraft thousands of metres overhead. They got out the torch and flashed it. Although not very hopeful, it was still worth a try. By this stage, they were cramped, cold and bored. They talked about the people in the jet and mused that they too would be short of leg room. They were at the end of their fourth day. They hadn't expected the wait to be so long and were now being very careful with their remaining rations. Realising that it could be an awful lot longer before they were spotted, they had a serious talk about the situation. Dabbs wished he had told the radio operator that they were actually getting into the life raft. Without this knowledge, he felt sure that the RAAF would soon abandon the search. They recorded their thoughts in the raft's log book. They reflected on their own situation and wondered what would happen to their families. Another night passed.

Although the aircraft heard by the survivors that Tuesday afternoon had not sighted them, it had discovered traces of the *One and All*. Ninety nautical miles from the last radioed position, one of the RAAF Orion crews spotted a plastic bottle, a hatch cover and some planks. It seemed like treasure trove. This discovery was made at 3.00 p.m. The search was to be abandoned at 5.00 p.m. but at last there were signs that people might still be alive. The aircraft crew dropped delayed action flares alongside the debris to guide vessels to the correct location. The *Otway, Edison* and *Lang* immediately headed towards the area at full speed.

On Tuesday Jack Kenny's wife, Anne, had heard a rumour that the search would be called off that afternoon. The Kennys had five children; the eldest was 15 years old and the youngest was only eight months. Anne Kenny was frantic. She knew that the life raft on the ketch contained rations for a week and she had an overpowering feeling that the crew of the *One and All* was still alive. The thought that the search might be called off when they were out there somewhere on the water was unbearable. Anne Kenny sent two telegrams; one to Prime Minister, William McMahon and the second to Navy Minister, Dr Mackay. The telegrams both carried the same message, 'For God's sake continue search for seven Christian souls and for the sake of our five children.'

Right behind Anne Kenny were the members of the women's group, CARP (Campaign Against Rising Prices). The CARP spokeswoman pointed out that much more time and money had been spent searching for former Prime Minister, Harold Holt, who had disappeared in the ocean. Surely seven ordinary people were at least worth as much as a missing Prime Minister? Anne Kenny, along with Marie Collins, mother of Margaret Collins, also paid a visit to Queensland Premier, Joh Bjelke Petersen. They told the Premier that they were sure the crew were still alive, and that the search had to go on. The women begged him to intervene and prevent the search from being cancelled. The Premier pledged his help and called the Prime Minister.

The sighting of the debris, the telegrams, and the Premier's call were enough to postpone the abandonment of the search. Next morning, at daybreak, the aircraft were out searching again. They swept back and forth over the area, relentlessly combing the surface of the water for anything that would lead them to the survivors. The HMAS *Otway* retrieved some of the debris which had been spotted the previous day. It was a piece of fibreboard panelling, painted white on one side. It matched the panelling of the *One and All* and was the first real indicator of the ketch's presence in these waters. The search was extended to an area 125 nautical miles north of Middleton Reef. The HMAS *Otway* and two RAAF Neptunes would search an area of 4800 square nautical miles.

On board the life raft, Wednesday came and went. The seven survivors were allowing themselves 113 millilitres of water four times a day, savouring each cool, fresh drop. Their emergency rations, the food tablets and compressed biscuits, were fast diminishing. The Brylcreem that was the cause of much derision upon its discovery that first day in the life raft, had been put to good use. They rubbed it on their sore and chaffed bottoms, which had resulted from sitting endlessly in the same position in the wet. They didn't have slicked down hair, but they all avoided salt burns! They still managed to maintain the hourly watch but were constantly drifting in and out of sleep. Dehydration, hunger and cramps were taking hold of them. As the hours ticked away, they began to feel increasingly uncomfortable about the sharks cruising around the life raft.

Late in the day they heard more aircraft noises. They wondered whether they were search aircraft, or whether the search for them had ended. They couldn't see any aircraft and knew they were much too far away to risk wasting a precious flare. Night came and there was no more aircraft noise and no sign of ships. They were quite sure now that all attempts to find them had been stopped, and each one wrote a final farewell message in the log book.

Thursday was day six. They had attempted to stay in one position to increase their chances of being found. Certain that the search had been called off, they now decided to try the idea of sailing. They still had a little food and enough water for ten more days, and they had not thrown anything out of the raft. They spent the day turning the raft into a boat. The long, strong tube of cardboard which had contained the raft kit was about 65 centimetres in diameter. They squashed it flat, rolled it into a solid pole, bandaged it tightly and varnished it with Friars Balsam to turn it into a makeshift mast. They tied a paddle to it to form a cross arm and put up a sail made from a spray jacket. All the empty food tins and cartons were tied into a U shaped plastic bag to become a lee board. This enabled them to sail across the wind. The survivors of the *One and All* were about 300 nautical miles from land, but every mile they sailed would bring them nearer to the shipping lanes, and increase their chances of being found. Taking things into their own hands, they were now very optimistic they would survive.

As the day wore on, the weather deteriorated. The sea was getting stronger and the wind was increasing as they headed into their sixth night. The light was fading when Margaret Collins heard an aircraft. Her long distance hearing was acute and she had always been first to pick up the aircraft sounds. Then the others heard the sound of aircraft engines coming closer. This sounded as though it might be worth a flare. It was getting on for 6.30 p.m. when they threw back the flaps of the raft and Kenny let off a parachute flare.

Piloted by Flight Lieutenant Arthur Shorthouse, the Neptune Rescue 133 was just about to wind up the search for the day and head back to Amberley Air Base, south-west of Brisbane. They had been searching an area 150 nautical miles away and this was the final search flight. The operator radioed the search centre in Penrith, west of Sydney, to inform them that the Neptune Rescue 133 was pulling out of the area. Arthur Shorthouse started to put the Neptune into a climb from their search level of about 300 metres. As they rose up to 1060 metres, both Shorthouse and his co-pilot gasped in amazement. Ahead of them they saw a red flare light shoot up. 'I think we've got it!' yelled Shorthouse. The message was relayed to the HMAS *Otway* and from there to search headquarters. Shorthouse then arranged for a smoke light to be dropped from the aircraft. Commander Roach of the HMAS *Otway* took the position fix from the Neptune and set the submarine towards the estimated location at maximum speed.

As they set off the flare the crew of the *One and All* experienced a mixture of joy and panic. There was only room for one of them at the canopy of the raft and Kenny was there waving the torch. Inside the life raft, the others could hear the Neptune growing closer by the minute until it was actually overhead. Above them, Shorthouse and his crew could see the orange lifeboat and a lone man standing at the entrance, waving a torch. It was impossible to tell whether there were other people in the raft but at least they had found one survivor.

The crew of Rescue 133 was elated. They had been flying shifts for 175 hours and finally, just 51 nautical miles from Middleton Reef, 40 nautical miles from the *One and All*'s last radioed position, they had spotted survivors. The aircraft was low on fuel and had to head back to base, so they dropped a marker beacon and flare to help the second search aircraft, Neptune Rescue 134, which was trailing not far behind. As Shorthouse turned his aircraft back, Rescue 134 arrived at the location and began to circle the raft.

The seven people on board were overwhelmed with a sense of relief that bordered on hysteria. They had been spotted! They knew it would be some time yet before they would be plucked out of the water, but the Neptune circling overhead assured them of their rescue. The Neptune crew now began the delicate job of dropping two rubber life rafts that would inflate on contact with the surface of the water. It was essential that they landed close enough to the survivors' location so they could grab hold of them. Circling as low and as slowly as safely possible, the pilot brought the aircraft close to the required position and made the drop. Two new life rafts fell on the correct drift line. Perfect! The Neptune dropped a marine flare which would ignite two hours after hitting the water. This ensured that they would still have a mark on the life rafts when darkness fell.

The crew of *One and All* were ecstatic. They paddled wildly through the big waves, shipping water in their excitement. The Neptune kept dropping flares and circling as the crew finally caught hold of one of the dropped life rafts and tied it to their own. As fast as they safely could, they piled into the new raft. Designed for ten people, there was plenty of room and lots of water, food and chocolate. There was even the joy of cigarettes for those who were smokers! Enormously relieved, they ate, drank and smoked, and intermittently flashed their torch to the Neptune circling overhead.

As the RAAF kept watch on the survivors, the submarine HMAS *Otway* was on her way to rescue them. Commander Terry Roach was prepared for a very delicate operation. He was 22 crew members short and the submarine was not a vessel designed for rescue work. By 11.00 p.m. the HMAS *Otway* was still 20 nautical miles away. Commander Roach was estimating his arrival time at 12.30 a.m.: sure enough, by 12.34 a.m. the raft was in her sights, and a great cheer went up. Through the darkness, the survivors saw the *Otway*'s lights approaching. They strained their eyes to try and work out what kind of vessel was coming to rescue them.

On board the submarine, Lieutenant Rick Canham and Able Seaman 'Shorty' Needham were in their diving gear. They were ready to go into the water to bring the dinghy up to the submarine. Canham was trained in handling underwater emergencies and Commander Roach and he agreed that the safest way to deal with the situation was for the divers to haul the raft alongside the submarine. The divers would also set up handrails to help the survivors and other *Otway* crew keep their balance on the surface of the submarine. Roach was deeply concerned about the operation. Apart from needing to ensure the safety of the *One and All* survivors whose condition he was unsure of, he was also anxious to ensure the safety of his crew who would need to go above on the submarine—the seas were strong and he feared crew members might be washed overboard.

An RAAF Orion had joined the rescue and as the HMAS *Otway* neared the life raft, the Orion's searchlights were switched to full beam. The crew of the submarine could see the seven people in the raft waving to them. Divers Canham and Needham slipped into the water and made their way towards the raft, while the crew on board brought the submarine into a safe position alongside *Otway*.

It took only 40 minutes from the time the *One and All* crew spotted the lights of the submarine until they were all on board. Guided by the two navy divers, each person was brought to the side of the submarine. They were hauled up onto it by the *Otway* crew, who were also struggling to stay upright on the rolling submarine. By 1.10 a.m. the survivors were safely on board, lying on bunks, dressed in warm clothes and drinking sweet tea and cocoa. It had been a week since they had left Middleton Reef—a week in which they experienced the terror of a storm which had sunk their ketch, and a six-day vigil in a cramped life raft. Now, on their way to Sydney, they could at last relax.

With the exception of Dabbs and Kenny, the crew of the *One and All* were not experienced sailors. Yet they demonstrated discipline and seamanship of an extremely high standard, and it was this that saved their lives. Their ability to follow instructions, work together and stay calm kept them safe and alive in circumstances which would have inspired panic and hysteria in many others. Truly outstanding was the rescue by the HMAS *Otway*. Commander Terry Roach and divers Canham and Needham demonstrated exceptional courage and seamanship in a delicate rescue operation, Australia's first and only rescue by submarine.

The story of the sinking of the *One and All* and her crew's six-day ordeal in the raft held the media headlines for days. While the crew were in the raft there had been extensive speculation about the real purpose of the voyage. There was talk of drug smuggling and of plans to establish an offshore gambling facility. Yet 26 years later, Peter Dabbs explains it very simply. The incident occurred just after attempts to search for oil on the Great Barrier Reef had been banned by the Australian Government. An associate of Dabbs' had been flying over Middleton Reef around that time and was contemplating its exploration. He later discovered that there was no ownership claim on the reef. A syndicate was formed and an international claim lodged for the State of Middleton. With the possibility of oil and the probability of natural gas in the area, arrangements were made with an oil company to begin a search. Dabbs' contract was to set up the beacon as a reference point for seismic surveys.

But another mystery surrounds the rescue of the crew of the *One and All*. Before abandoning ship Peter Dabbs radioed their final position to Brisbane—the crew was found only 40 nautical miles from that location, and only 51 nautical miles from Middleton Reef. So why did it take six days and a search over thousands of miles to locate the raft? To this day the question remains unanswered.

Like the very best adventure stories, that of the *One and All* also has a happy ending. Peter Dabbs and Margaret Collins had gone to sea as colleagues and emerged from their ordeal as good friends. They stayed in touch and their friendship grew into romance. 'We decided if we could spend a week together on a life raft, we ought to be able to get on all right together on land,' Dabbs says. The pair continued working together and were married a few years later. They now live in Queensland with their two daughters, and are still enthusiastic sailors.

Rescuing the Rescuers

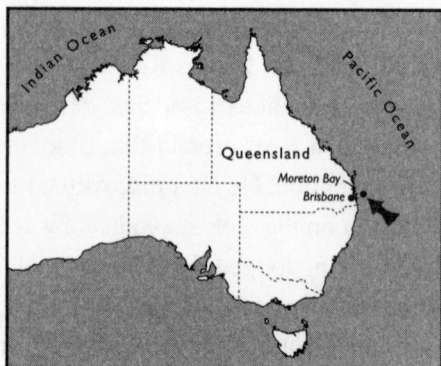

Rescue of the crew from the *Leigh* and two
members of the Redcliffe Volunteer Coast
Guard, Moreton Bay, Queensland,
9 May 1980.

*'When I was under the water I thought, this
is it—I'm gone!'* Malcolm Dixon.

Cheryl Manton was looking forward to seeing her
parents. For two years she and her partner, Malcolm
Dixon, and their two-year-old daughter, Leigh, had been
living aboard their eight-metre sloop, the *Leigh*, and
sailing the east coast of Australia. They were on a five-
year dream cruise to the Barrier Reef and were planning
to meet Cheryl's parents on the Sunshine Coast. It was
some time since they had all been together and as well
as the excitement of the reunion, Cheryl, who was now
five months pregnant with her second child, was also
looking forward to a spell on dry land. Two years at sea

had not cured her of sea sickness and the *Leigh* had been rocking all night.

The *Leigh* was a Spacesailer 27, designed in Western Australia by Kim Swabrick. Originally named *Strider* she had proved herself in Sydney ocean races and was extremely well equipped with top of the range electronic instruments, winches, a Seafarer depths sounder and a good sail area. With a bright red hull and 1364 kilograms of ballast in her lead keel, this tough and reliable boat was the ideal yacht for Dixon and Manton to turn their dream cruise into reality.

The couple had sheltered overnight in the quiet waters of Bulwer Bay behind Bribie Island, 20 kilometres north of Brisbane. That Friday morning, 9 May 1980, they were to head up the coast to Mooloolaba for the planned holiday. As the family ate their breakfast, the weather in the bay was calm. But Malcolm Dixon could see signs which made him cautious. After breakfast he listened to the weather forecast, checked his charts, and looked out from the deck. There was quite a swell around the Comboyuro Point and as he watched grey clouds rolling overhead, he knew they were in for high seas. The forecast predicted south-south-easterly winds up to 30 knots and rough seas with a moderate to heavy swell. There was also a strong wind warning for the region and a warning of thunderstorms south of Moreton Island.

Dixon double-checked the charts and the forecast. He was a thoughtful and intelligent sailor in a well-equipped boat, and was not about to take any risks with the lives of those nearest and dearest to him. He decided the trip through the North East Channel would mean a rough start, but once they reached the open sea, with the wind behind them, the *Leigh* would be in ideal conditions. Malcolm Dixon predicted that the strong winds would take them swiftly through to Mooloolaba.

They decided to leave at 8.00 a.m., timing the departure so that they could head out of the North East Channel as the tide turned. The initial rough conditions were not ideal but Dixon reckoned they were manageable. He began to rig the *Leigh* with a small genoa sail which would best suit the weather he anticipated meeting when they were out on the open sea. After two years at sea, the couple made an efficient team. They weighed anchor on time, with Dixon at the helm and Manton watching the charts. Down below, little Leigh played in her bunk.

While the family on the *Leigh* made their plans for the voyage, the Flotilla Commander of the Redcliffe branch of the Australian Volunteer Coast Guard was on his way to his day job. Vern Bunter was a carpenter working on a contract for cottage frames for a new suburban estate. With his colleague, Colin Ward, the two men were hoping to make progress on a contract that was already delayed. The weather didn't look at all promising but they were off to an early start.

Bunter and Ward were colleagues at work and also at sea. In his early twenties, Colin Ward was an experienced member of the 70-strong Redcliffe squadron. The two men would often drop their tools and make the run back to Bunter's home to pick up the Coast Guard's Sharkcat in response to a call for help from leisure yachts in Moreton

1. *Shelley Boy* skipper, Robert Line (right), with HMAS *Junee* crew.

2. HMAS *Fremantle* heads to the sinking cray-fishing boat, *Shelley Boy*.

3. Survivors of the *Noongah* board the Japanese tanker, *Koyo Maru*.

4. The crew of the *One and All* rescued by the submarine, HMAS *Otway*.

5. Commander Terry Roach of HMAS *Otway* (right) and Peter Dabbs.

Above 6. The Redcliffe Volunteer Coast Guard's Sharkcat is flipped in the rough seas.
Left 7. Vern Bunter hangs on to the rail of the Channel 0 Eye Witness News helicopter.

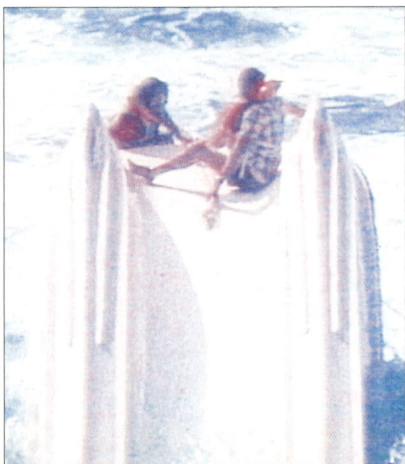

8. Colin Ward and Vern Bunter cling to the upturned Sharkcat.

9. Coast Guards Ward and Bunter climb onto the helicopter.

10. The *Leigh*, caught by the huge wave that rolled her.

11. Although her crew were unharmed, the *Leigh* suffered a broken mast.

12. A trawler from the Kailis France fleet washed up after Cyclone Kathy.

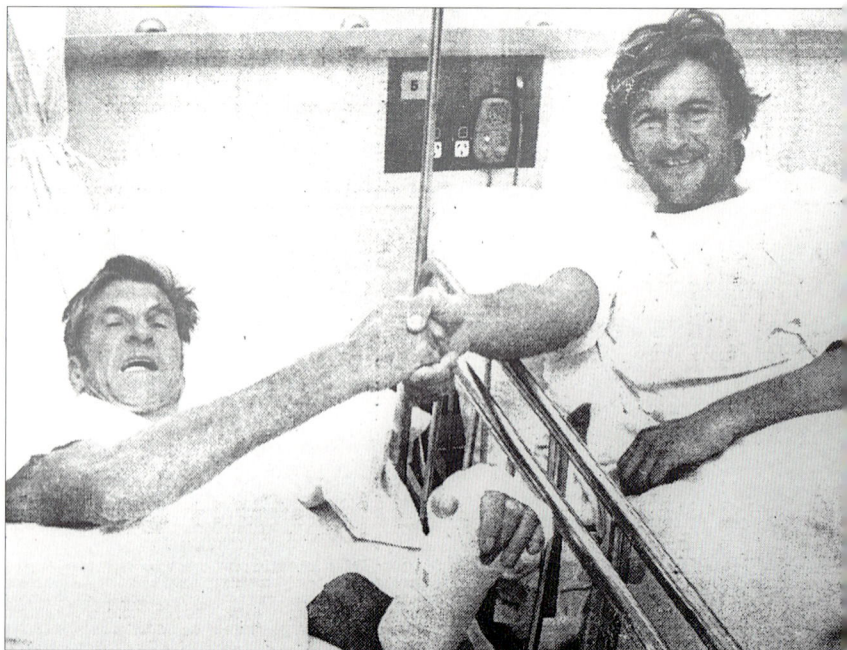

13. A relieved Julian Martin (right) and Reg Bladwell from the *Moana Ari*.

4. Lyn, Bryce and Stephen Quarrie before their trip on the *Tiraumea*.

5. The *Tiraumea* a 13-metre centre-board yacht.

16. Roger Meadmore tries to land his balloon on the deck of the *Apex 11*.

17. The balloon basket hits the water and skids along at a speed of 15 knots.

Bay. Working hand-in-hand with the police, the Redcliffe Squadron covers a territory from the south of Moreton Island north to Caloundra Head.

In the morning's bleak and unseasonal weather, the Brisbane Water Police started work. It looked like the weather would remain rough all day. Rain squalls driven by a cold, south-easterly wind were sweeping through the city and the forecast was gloomy. A low pressure cell off the coast was whipping up heavy seas and stronger winds were on the way. Senior Constables Bob Harding and Neville Cooper were no strangers to days like these or the subsequent calls of help they were anticipating. Experience, however, did not make them careless and they meticulously carried out the standard equipment check of the *G. J. Olive*, the Water Police's seven-metre Sharkcat.

Sea rescues are the everyday work of the Water Police. They know their designated stretch of coast like the backs of their hands and never underestimate nature's potential to turn on the unexpected challenge. From pulling a small boat out of the shallows or checking reports of suspicious activity, to saving lives at sea, the Water Police, like their colleagues the Volunteer Coast Guard, go to the aid of hundreds of vessels every year.

Malcolm Dixon and Cheryl Manton made their way past the first couple of buoys and headed down the channel to the open sea. To the north there seemed to be some improvement in the weather. The skies were clearing and there was even a bit of sunshine coming through. The swell was still strong though and Dixon maintained his sense of caution. His rigging was deliberately conservative. As he continued on, leaving behind the shelter of the bay, his sense of unease grew—the weather, the swell, it just didn't seem quite right. The waves were getting bigger. Many were breaking across the deck of the *Leigh* and she was pitching in the strong water. It was enough to make Dixon worried about his original plan and he decided to bring the yacht about.

As he slowly completed the manoeuvre he was shocked to see an enormous wave heading towards him. This was far bigger than anything he'd seen before and the *Leigh* was right in its path. A tower of water was racing towards him, breaking white across the top and foaming as it tumbled down the great curve. It crashed against the *Leigh* beam on, and hurled the yacht over until the top of the mast pitched down into the water and the boat was driven fast along by the force of the water.

Dixon was thrown overboard from the deck. As he struggled wildly for the surface, he was thankful for the harness holding him to the boat and dragging him alongside. Down below, Cheryl Manton and Leigh were thrown together. Only their harnesses limited the distance they travelled, as the cupboards spewed their contents and kitchen utensils and crockery flew around the cabin. The portable television was hurled from its fixing and the fridge broke free from its housing and crashed onto the floor. Water was pouring into the cabin from the companionway.

As the *Leigh* righted herself from the knock down, she lost her sail. At the same time, the anchor hatch was ripped off by the force of the water and great lengths of anchor warp fell away into the ocean. Surfacing alongside his yacht, Dixon struggled to drag himself back on board. He was desperate to see what had happened to Cheryl and Leigh. He found them huddled together, shaken but uninjured, amid the chaos of the flooded cabin.

Dixon knew he must head back for the channel. But just as quickly as the single cylinder diesel engine fired to life, it died away again. Then he noticed the anchor rope trailing out from his boat and tangled in the propeller. The knock down had torn it out of the hatch and curling metres of warp were afloat. The *Leigh* was now drifting rapidly out of the channel into huge waves crashing up over the shallows. Despite the huge waters, there was not enough wind to sail out of trouble. Malcolm Dixon knew the situation was bad. With the propeller fouled, the anchor warp trailing in the water, and the genoa sail gone, there was no alternative but to make a mayday call.

Colin Ward was listening to the news. His early morning start had fizzled out when the materials he and Vern Bunter needed for the job failed to arrive. The foul weather made other work on the cottage frames impossible and Bunter had dropped him back at home. As Ward sat sipping his coffee and contemplating the rest of the day, he switched on the radio for the ten o'clock news. Malcolm Dixon had made his distress call at 9.52 a.m. and already it was in the bulletin. 'A yacht in distress in the North East Channel,' the newsreader reported. Ward turned down the volume and telephoned Vern Bunter, telling him that the Water Police might be needing some help from the Coast Guard.

Within ten minutes, Vern Bunter had confirmed the situation with the Water Police, hitched up the Sharkcat and was on his way to pick up Ward. The two men were in the water, 16 nautical miles from the location of the *Leigh*, even before the official police call to the Redcliffe Volunteer Coast Guard had been made. The Coast Guard radio station, housed in a caravan at the boat ramp, was open and search coordinators Arthur Wessels and Roy King were in charge.

Also on the way was the Water Police's *G. J. Olive*, racing towards the *Leigh* at 45 knots. Bob Harding and Neville Cooper had a long way to go. They had a 12-nautical-mile run to Moreton Bay, then another 25 nautical miles to cross the bay. Even if they maintained speed, it would still take them three quarters of an hour to get to the *Leigh*. It was an appalling day and Cooper and Harding knew that a yacht in trouble out there was in really big trouble. They both knew that the Volunteer Coast Guard's Sharkcat would reach the *Leigh* before them, and hoped it would be soon enough to avert a disaster.

Bunter and Ward were making good headway full speed across the bay. Within about six nautical miles of their target, they could see what was lying ahead. As the bay opened to the sea there was a mass of white water. Sailing closer, they began to feel the impact of the growing height and frequency of the swell. The conditions slowed them down from 50 knots to about 18 knots, but the Sharkcat ploughed on. Cutting through the huge waters, Ward and Bunter were blinded by the spray and foam. Although they were highly experienced sailors and had gone to the aid of hundreds of yachts in terrible conditions, Bunter and Ward had never encountered the sea as it was that day.

The huge seas also slowed down the Water Police. As

they tried to make their way out through the North East Channel, Harding and Cooper were horrified at the monstrous size of the waves. The *G. J. Olive* climbed the towering waves at a 45 degree angle, crashing through the dense mass of water. It was just over an hour since the *Leigh*'s distress call had been picked up. Overhead, the Water Police saw the BTQ Channel 7 helicopter signalling at them to continue further out to sea. As they battled on, a radio message gave them the location for the distressed yacht. It was still ten nautical miles away. Just like Bunter and Ward, the Water Police were hoping to catch sight of their target but the seas were so huge and the spray so dense that it was impossible.

The crew of the *Leigh* knew that help was on the way. But as the waters continued to pound their yacht, they wondered if it would be soon enough. Against all the odds, the *Leigh* was still afloat; she had taken three more knock downs since the mayday call just before 10.00 a.m. and it was now 10.45 a.m. They were at the point of exhaustion, just hanging on. Through the waves they could see sharks in the water, a constant reminder of the danger of their situation. Malcolm Dixon had managed to cut away the warp and free the rudder, but the propeller was still fouled and would not turn. He was at the helm and was bending his head down to the cabin to warn Cheryl of another huge wave approaching when, to his huge relief, he spotted the Volunteer Coast Guard's Sharkcat bursting fiercely through the waves.

As Dixon sighed with relief, the media helicopters above were busy filming the scene for the nation's evening news bulletins. The Channel 0 Eye Witness News chopper had been first to reach the scene. Mark Nichols, the cameraman on board, was filming as the pilot, Tom Ward, an ex-RAAF veteran who had seen service in Vietnam, took stock of the situation. The Channel 0 helicopter was on loan from Wales Surf Rescue and was not carrying the sophisticated ENG (electronic news gathering) equipment that a television news helicopter would normally have on board. This meant that Tom Ward could carry a couple of passengers back to shore if necessary. But as he saw the Volunteer Coast Guard closing in on the *Leigh*, it seemed as though that sort of help would not be necessary.

The Channel 0 helicopter was soon joined by the BTQ Channel 7 chopper, packed with ENG equipment and piloted by Greg Rogers, an ex-navy pilot. John Heselwood, the cameraman on board, had filmed some stunning footage of the *Leigh* and now both he and the cameraman from the Channel 0 helicopter were filming the Coast Guard's Shark-cat as it came into view. Suddenly three massive, freak waves broke out of the main swell and roared across the channel towards the *Leigh*. With cameras whirring, the helicopter crews watched in amazement.

Malcolm Dixon had been looking out towards the Shark-cat. He heard the roaring water behind him and swung to face it. There was no time to turn the *Leigh* around before the first huge wave bore down on the yacht. The wave hurled the *Leigh* over onto her side. As the mast pitched below the water, the yacht rolled a full and dramatic 360 degrees. The boat shuddered in a crashing somersault.

Dixon was hurled into the water. He was still harnessed

to the boat, but as he twisted and flew the rope of his harness wrapped around his neck, almost strangling him as he was dumped and then dragged in the roll. Under the water he fought for his life. Using both hands to wrench at the rope, he managed to loosen its grip around his neck and rose spluttering up to the surface. Through the waves he could see that the *Leigh*'s solid lead keel had swung her back into an upright position. She had broken her mast in the roll over but the rest of her was intact. Still struggling for his life, Dixon grasped at the rails. With a superb effort he dragged himself up from the water and back on to his rocking yacht.

The helicopter crews above watched in amazement as Dixon surfaced, struggled back on board and into the *Leigh*'s cockpit. They could see no sign of Cheryl Manton or her daughter. They didn't know whether the two were still inside the cabin or had been thrown out in the dramatic roll. But back on board, Dixon, deeply shocked and dazed by the dumping, saw that Cheryl and Leigh had survived the brutal roll with nothing more than a scratch.

In the Sharkcat, Ward and Bunter had seen the *Leigh* roll under the onslaught of the first freak wave. The Sharkcat managed to drop back down after the first huge wave had passed them. When the second wave reared up, Bunter accelerated to bring the boat up and through it. The boat was facing slightly away from head on and was caught up in the hollow tube. When the boat broke through to the trough, water drowned the entire boat and cut out the port motor. Now the Sharkcat had only 50 per cent of its power and the third monstrous wave was bearing down on it.

Bunter tried to bring the boat about but the loss of power had crippled her and she was caught beam on and thrown onto her side. The starboard bow rose almost vertically in the air before the boat fell backwards and rolled over under the pressure of the water. Colin Ward realised that there was nowhere else to go. As he wondered how they would get out of the situation, he was dumped into the water. Seconds later, Bunter, who had been clinging to the helm, was dumped too. The two men struggled furiously as the Sharkcat rolled over on top of them and trapped them in an air pocket. They knew the air would not last long and they thrashed their way out from under the Sharkcat, their two heads bobbing up above the water almost simultaneously. As they swam out, Bunter was able to grasp the floating anchor line and secure it to the towing eye, and the two men used the line to drag themselves up onto the upturned twin hulls of their boat.

As the camera crews filmed from the helicopters above, it soon became clear that the greatest danger was to Bunter and Ward. The *Leigh* was dismasted and pitching in the waves, but her crew was comparatively safe. Bunter and Ward, however, were perched perilously on the hull of the Sharkcat and were in danger of being washed off and lost in the swell.

Neither of the two helicopters had lifting gear, but Tom Ward in the Channel 0 chopper knew that he had the space to carry two passengers. The water was far too wild for the chopper to hover directly above its surface but Ward thought he should at least try to lift the two men off the upturned Sharkcat. Mark Nichols was still filming probably the most dramatic footage of his career when Ward motioned for him to put down his camera and help. He was going to try and position the chopper close enough to the upturned Sharkcat so that the two men could scramble aboard.

Close by in the Channel 7 helicopter, John Heselwood was still filming as Tom Ward took the Channel 0 aircraft down near the water. Vern Bunter and Colin Ward were slithering about dangerously as the upturned hull of the Sharkcat was thrown and dropped by the waves. They had no idea what the helicopter pilot was trying to do, and were wondering how in hell they were going to get out of this situation. The boat was riding up at least four and a half metres with every swell. Then Colin Ward realised that Mark Nichols was leaning out of the chopper, gesturing at them to grab the rails.

The intrepid, veteran pilot dropped the helicopter almost to the surface of the water, just after a wave passed. Colin Ward thrust forward and grasped the skid rail as the helicopter skipped up to miss an oncoming wave. But his grip slipped and he dropped off the skid rail into the water. Ward scrambled back up onto the upturned Sharkcat and, as the helicopter dropped down again, he caught the chopper's rail. This time, he managed to get a more secure grip and, as Tom Ward dodged the waves, the young Coast Guard scrambled into the safety of the helicopter.

Bunter was still on the upturned hull and Tom Ward dropped the helicopter down again to give him a chance to climb on. This time, the task seemed even more difficult as the upturned Sharkcat was riding high on a wave with breakers crashing across her. Ward tried to close in on the boat to give Bunter the best chance of clambering on the skid rail. Twice the rail hit the Sharkcat, but on the third attempt Ward positioned the helicopter close enough for Bunter to grab the rail. As he hung there perilously Tom Ward lifted the chopper away from the water and Mark Nichols dragged Bunter into the helicopter. The rescuers were rescued.

As the Eye Witness News helicopter banked to head back for land, Neville Cooper and Bob Harding arrived at the scene of the *Leigh* in the police boat. They had seen the extraordinary helicopter manoeuvre lifting the two men from the Sharkcat and were now concentrating on the rescue of the *Leigh*'s crew. The seas were moderating slightly, but the wind and waves were still huge as the Water Police brought the *G. J. Olive* as close as they could to the distressed yacht to secure a tow line. It was now 11.30 a.m., just over an hour and a half since Malcolm Dixon had sent out his distress call.

It had seemed like a lifetime, but finally the *Leigh* was back on her way to safety behind the *G. J. Olive*. As the two boats moved into the calmer waters of Moreton Bay, Cooper and Harding slowed the police boat to enable Cheryl Manton and her daughter to transfer out of the flooded cabin and into the *G. J. Olive*. When the yacht rolled, Cheryl and Leigh had been thrown around the cabin like dolls and hit by flying pots, pans, crockery and other objects. But despite this, the two were in amazingly good shape. An exhausted Malcolm Dixon stayed on the *Leigh* until they reached Bribie Island. He had been dumped in the ocean three times, had survived four knock downs and a roll over, and had very nearly drowned. Around his neck was the ugly rope burn from his harness, another reminder of his close brush with death.

When the Channel 0 Eye Witness News helicopter had set out that morning to collect news footage of the rescue, her pilot and cameraman never imagined they would abandon the news gathering to save two lives under the most extraordinary circumstances. The skill Tom Ward displayed in bringing his aircraft close enough to the upturned Shark-cat remains one of the finest acts of flying in rescue history. And Mark Nichols forfeited the most spectacular footage of any rescue on record in order to help save the lives of two Coast Guards. John Heselwood, the cameraman aboard the Channel 7 helicopter, continued filming alongside the Channel 0 helicopter, and that evening the stunning rescue footage was flashed across television screens all over the country.

Malcolm Dixon, Cheryl Manton and baby Leigh were taken to Bribie Island for a medical check. Leigh seemed unperturbed by her adventure and was keen to go home to the yacht. These days she remembers little of the incident except her father shouting to them as they sheltered in the cabin. Cheryl gave birth to a healthy daughter four months later, and the couple now have two more children. The family still enjoys sailing.

The two Coast Guards disembarked from the Channel 0 helicopter, hale and hearty, at Bribie Island. A medical check-up revealed that they had not even sustained a scratch throughout their ordeal. Vern Bunter has now retired, but

Colin Ward is still a keen and active member of the Redcliffe Volunteer Coast Guard. He continues to venture out in all kinds of weather to help rescue those in trouble. 'It's what we're there for,' he says laconically. But he does acknowledge that the rescue that day in May, 1980, was the most dramatic one. While he has seen similar weather conditions, boats and equipment have improved vastly, making rescue operations very different today.

Vern Bunter, Colin Ward, cameraman Mark Nichols, and Senior Constables Neville Cooper and Bob Harding all received bronze medals for bravery from the Royal Humane Society. Helicopter pilot Tom Ward was awarded a silver medal, which he did not accept. For the Vietnam veteran it was all in a day's work.

Battling a Cyclone

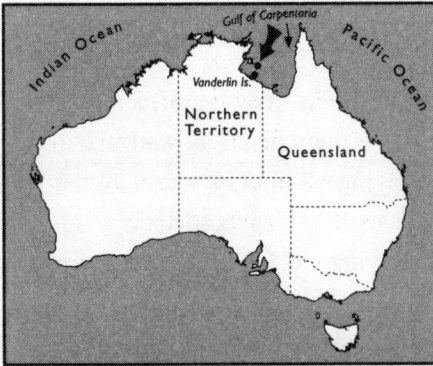

The rescue of five crew from the KVF prawn
trawler the *Lindeman* off Vanderlin Island,
Gulf of Carpentaria, 22 March 1984.

*'I knew you'd find me Sam—have you got a
beer?'* Nigel Robinson, mate from the
Lindeman.

The skipper of the *Comac Endeavour* had decided to
trust his own judgement and head out into the weather.
Cyclone Kathy's winds were raging at 160 knots and the
sea was full of islands and rocks. He wanted to get out
where there was room to move. None of his navigation aids
were working and he could not even see the bow of his own
boat. Richard 'Sam' Samuels had been on boats since he
was eight years old but he had never experienced winds like
these. They had knocked him down several times, but in
the wheelhouse he still felt in control of the situation.

Down below there was a hell of a noise. Unsure of what

was happening, Samuels put the mate on the wheel and went down to investigate. He discovered the domestic deep freeze had broken loose and, as the boat rocked furiously in the wind, the freezer was careering around from one side of the boat to the other. The five crew members sat around the galley table with their heads bowed and hands clasped— they were praying. Samuels wrestled the freezer down, secured it and took a long hard look at his terrified crew. 'Don't start praying 'til I do,' he ordered and headed back to the wheelhouse.

It was the beginning of the 1984 banana prawn fishing season in the Northern Prawn Fisheries. The Fisheries are the home of a $200 million industry and banana prawns comprise about 50 per cent of its revenue. With a healthy local market and a huge export market in Europe, Japan and the USA, the banana prawn season is vitally important for those who make their living in the Northern Prawn Fisheries.

Twenty of the 36 Kailis France (KFV) boats, Australia's largest prawn trawler fleet, were anchored off Vanderlin Island in the Gulf of Carpentaria. They had been assembled for a pre-season strategy meeting, a team-building exercise in which the planning and organisation for the coming banana prawn season would be laid down. The meeting was headed by the fleet masters, experienced skippers who had moved into management, and it was attended by the trawler skippers and their crews. Troubleshooters were out on the trawlers, inspecting them to make sure there were no problems with equipment. It was important that each vessel was operating efficiently and was well prepared for the start of the season. At the meeting one executive commented, 'Statistically, we're due to get wiped out by a cyclone.' A few days later he would be regretting his words.

The region had been under pressure from cyclones for a couple of weeks. At the beginning of March, Cyclone Ferdinand had swept across the coast of the Northern Territory. This was followed by Cyclone Jim, which had moved in from the Coral Sea and was heading across the Gulf to Roper River. Further north-east, Cyclone Kathy was forming. On 18 March, Cyclone Kathy moved across into the Gulf of Carpentaria. By Wednesday, 21 March, the cyclone was located in the centre of the Gulf and was steadily building in strength. She began moving to the southern coast of the Gulf, heading for the Sir Edward Pellew Islands. Vanderlin Island is the largest of these.

Seventeen of the KFV prawn fishing trawlers were anchored in the protection of Vanderlin Island's Geranium Bay, while three others were sheltering off Centre Island. At first it had seemed that Cyclone Kathy might just miss the islands but as time wore on, it became increasingly clear that the cyclone, described by the Bureau of Meteorology as 'very dangerous', was heading straight for the fleet.

The fleet masters decided to keep the ships together in an attempt to control what was likely to be a very dangerous situation. Chris Terjeson, skipper of the *Lindeman*, was one of three who had anchored off Centre Island. Together with the ship's mate, Nigel Robinson, the engineer, Mark Freeburg and the deckhand, Peter Lenehan, Terjeson took a final look over the boat to make sure everything was battened down. All the hatches were sealed, the awnings tied down, and everything moveable had been safely stowed away. Down below, the two cooks, Hillary Poole and Jeanette Newton, were stowing equipment and checking life jackets.

Prawn trawlers have very large booms and skippers vary in their opinions about how these should be handled in extreme weather conditions. While some skippers prefer to pull them in, others think there is a greater level of safety in leaving them out as they can stabilise the vessel. Terjeson held the latter view and left his booms out. Not far away from the *Lindeman*, the skipper of the *Orpheus*, Reg Brown, battened down, ensured that everything was as secure as possible and, like Terjeson, also kept his booms out.

Over in Geranium Bay, Richard Samuels was uneasy. He had pulled in his booms and filled the *Comac Endeavour* with brine to force her to sit low in the water. This would help stabilise the boat when the winds came. When he first became aware that a cyclone would hit the area, Samuels wanted to go out to sea. But understanding the concern of the fleet masters to keep the boats together, he battened down and stayed in the bay. He did move his boat further away from some of the other vessels, as he felt this would give him more space if the boats started to drag their anchors.

By late afternoon, Cyclone Kathy was making good speed towards the fleet. Checking the barometer Samuels saw the needle falling away rapidly. On the radar, the cyclone was showing up as a black hole surrounded by white and was tracking straight for their position. At first it didn't seem too bad. The wind picked up but it just felt like a very windy day. The boats were in a sheltered anchorage and the general feeling was that they would weather the effects of the cyclone.

By the time darkness fell Cyclone Kathy was still about 20 nautical miles away. Spread across the bay, the fleet of trawlers had time to prepare themselves and the skippers, their crews, the fleet masters and the troubleshooters were ready for the storm. But not even the most experienced of them was really prepared for what happened.

As the cyclone drew closer the winds kept increasing beyond anyone's expectations. They moved from storm to gale force, then to hurricane force. At one point, one of Samuels' crew had been up on deck to drop the anchor. As he was holding onto the T of the anchor, the wind whipped his legs from underneath him. For some moments the wind was blowing him in a horizontal position, his legs streaming out behind him. The wind had now reached the incredible level where anyone who ventured onto the deck would be blown overboard and it was accompanied by driving rain.

The reassuring sight of land and the other boats soon disappeared and some of the boats started to drag their anchors. Unable to see, the crews feared they would crash into each other or be dragged back onto the rocks around the bay. On some of the boats panic was breaking out and the skippers had their work cut out trying to calm younger and less experienced crew members.

Samuels pulled up the *Comac Endeavour*'s anchors and decided to head into the weather. The water was a minefield of rocks and islands. If he was going to hit something, he wanted to hit it head on so that he could use his propellers to get the boat off the rocks. He planned to move ahead of the weather and try and hold his position, rather than dragging backwards. To get out ahead of the weather he would have to dodge the rocks and islands. The spray and driving rain was whipping the boat about and he could not see the bow of his own vessel, let alone the surrounding rocks or other vessels. As the cyclone hit, all of the *Comac Endeavour*'s navigation instruments failed. When the barometer had dropped to its vertical downward position, the radar had also been rendered useless. The scanner on top of the trawler was being whirled around so fast by the wind that each time they tried to use it, it just blew out the fuse. The echo sounder, used for bottom definition, was useless.

Samuels had worked in far worse seas but he had never known wind like this. The sky seemed to sweep down to meet the water, creating a blinding fog. Visibility was practically nil and with so many boats anchored in the comparatively small bay, the chances of a collision were high. *Comac Endeavour* was an almost new, 23-metre trawler and she was taking a terrible hammering.

Over the radio, Samuels could hear the terrified confusion as some of the other skippers communicated with the fleet masters. There were screams of panic, people crying and desperate pleas for help. He wanted to get out of the area as fast as possible. He was starting to make a little headway when he heard the noise below and ran down to find his crew deep in prayer. After securing the freezer he went back up to the wheelhouse.

Samuels was pretty sure the situation on his boat was now under control and he wanted to take a look at the radar. With the mate on the wheel and himself at the radar, he gave Paul Green, one of the fleet's troubleshooters on board, the task of replacing the radar's fuses. Samuels felt that if he could get a full sweep on the radar, he would be able to find out if there were other boats near him and avoid any potential hazard in the water.

Paul Green must have renewed the fuses in the radar 40 times, but it was worth it. Several times they got a full sweep on the screen before the fuses blew, and this enabled Samuels to dodge the rocks and islands. Working together with Green and the mate, Samuels was able to navigate the *Comac Endeavour* through the rocks and head further out of the bay. Even so, it was extremely difficult to control the boat and she was constantly knocked down on her side. Each time she dropped the bilge alarms went off, which added to the terrifying cacophony of the storm. Water was making its way into the boat and there was nearly half a metre of it on the wheelhouse floor. Suddenly the winds dropped. They were on the edge of the eye of the cyclone. They could feel the pressure weighing them down and there was the terrifying knowledge that once they passed this temporary breathing space worse was to come.

Back in Geranium Bay, chaos reigned as more of the boats dragged their anchors and were blown back onto the beach or rocks. Off Centre Island the *Lindeman*, *Orpheus* and *Invincible II* were still taking a beating. The electrical and navigation equipment on the *Orpheus* had gone down and Reg Brown had no functioning radar or lights. Blinded by the rain and spray, the crew of the *Orpheus* were enveloped in darkness. It was impossible to send someone out on deck to check the situation because the winds were so strong and quite capable of ripping off a crew member's harness.

The *Lindeman*'s situation was even worse. The cyclone had hit the boat with tremendous force and she immediately began to drag her anchor. The trawler had been forced so far back that she had ploughed into the rocks, ripping a hole in her hull. She was taking on water fast and Chris Terjeson knew they were in severe trouble. All he could do was hope they would not sustain any more damage and that they could wait out the storm on the rocks. The crew was in darkness and the trawler was listing strongly, the list intensified by the driving force of the wind.

Taking stock of the situation, Terjeson decided that the galley was the safest part of the boat. It was also, at present, the driest. To attempt to get off the boat in the surrounding darkness would have been madness. The wind force was so intense and the pressure so great that it was doubtful if anyone could have breathed outside, let alone survived in the water. As Terjeson and his crew huddled together in the galley they found themselves in the eye of the cyclone. The air seemed charged with an immensely powerful force. The terrifying noise of the wind dropped and they were enveloped by an even more terrifying silence. A leaden silence. Sea birds fell dead from the sky into the water. It seemed like a long and sinister threat of what was to come.

Reg Brown decided to take advantage of the eye to head for safer waters. He pulled the *Orpheus*' anchors up and headed out in the direction of Walker Point. As he moved off he tried to reach Chris Terjeson on the radio, but by this time the crew of the *Lindeman* were huddled in the galley.

Reg Brown felt a huge responsibility to remain in control of his boat and stay calm in front of his crew. He had skippered the *Orpheus* for just a little over a year. Like most of the other skippers he had encountered huge seas with waves towering 20 metres and more off the Gulf of Carpentaria and on the other side of the continent off Tasmania—but nothing had prepared him for the fury of the cyclone's wind and the deep leaden stillness of its eye.

Terror struck Reg Brown's bones and he desperately wanted to make contact with the *Lindeman*. Its skipper, Chris Terjeson was an old friend and the two had spent the previous year together in the Philippines. As Brown headed out through the darkness he caught sight of the *Lindeman* impaled on the rocks. The sight ripped the breath from his lungs. The wind was working up again and Brown faced an agonising decision. He could keep going and try to get the *Orpheus* to a safer location where she could ride out the rest of the storm. Or he could attempt to reach the *Lindeman* and help his mate. He hung there for a precious moment in the agony of indecision, but deep down, he knew there was no real choice to be made. To risk heading for the *Lindeman* would be sheer madness. It would almost certainly result in the loss of his boat and crew, and his first responsibility was to them. Taking a final look at the *Lindeman* listing perilously on the rocks, Brown pushed on into safer waters—in the distance he could see *New Fish II* also dangerously close to the rocks. He was soon greeted by the phenomenal winds of Cyclone Kathy once more raging furiously around his boat.

The crew of *Comac Endeavour* had emerged from the

eerie stillness of the cyclone's eye, back into the raging turmoil of the winds. The trawler was taking regular knock downs, but Richard Samuels was still fairly confident that he could maintain the situation. Using all his power, Samuels headed straight into the wind. Each time he managed to turn the boat into the wind, she would be knocked down in the opposite direction. Samuels had ordered the booms to be pulled in just before the cyclone had hit, but the crew member who had performed the task was inexperienced and had put the stainless steel fixing pin in back to front.

As Samuels battled on full power to keep the *Comac Endeavour* head on to the wind, he heard the tremendous crash of the boom as it broke free of its fixings. The boom was swinging around wildly in the wind, but it was too dangerous to send someone out to secure it. They would either be hit by the boom or blown overboard. Samuels feared the boom would crash into the water, foul the propeller and they would end up on the beach or the rocks. The boom smashed about as the crew watched in terror to see where it would end. With an extraordinary stroke of luck, the great arm wrapped around and locked itself in place. Samuels thought to himself that maybe the crew's prayers had not been such a bad idea after all. He took a deep breath and continued heading the *Comac Endeavour* into the wind.

In the dark galley of the *Lindeman*, the crew had spent the last 20 minutes sitting out the eye of the cyclone. As Kathy swung around, it hit the boat from the opposite direction, ripped her off the rocks and tore a huge hole in the hull on the port side. The engine room flooded instantly and the galley rapidly began to fill with water. Chris Terjeson had hoped they would be able to stay on the boat and avoid the horrendous conditions outside. But now they had no choice. The water was rising around them and they had to get out of the galley as quickly as possible. They would have to swim through to the forepeak, away from the list which was dragging down the stern of the boat.

Terjeson urged the crew to make their way through the waterlogged boat. Alternately swimming and stumbling in the darkness, they had no idea how long their air would last. The water level was rising fast and they needed to get up into the forepeak as fast as possible. Terjeson wrenched open the hatch and the ship's mate, Nigel Robinson clambered up first, turning to pull cooks Hillary Poole and Jeanette Newton up into the focsle. Terjeson, engineer Freeburg and deckhand Lenehan kept swimming as the angle of the list increased. Freeburg and Lenehan were hauled out of the water and up into the forepeak as the boat sank lower, but Terjeson was left swimming frantically. There was now a very steep angle that Terjeson had to scale to get out of the water and into the forepeak space. He trod water desperately, trying to grab hold of Robinson's arm and haul himself up. But as much as they stretched the two men could not quite reach each other. If Terjeson didn't get up there quickly and shut the hatch it would be too late. He didn't think he could hang on much longer and every minute spent trying to get him out was increasing the risk for the rest of the crew. 'If you can't grab me next time you'd better close the hatch,' he yelled to Robinson.

Overwhelmed by exhaustion and the prospect of drowning in the dark cavern of the *Lindeman*'s hull, Terjeson summoned all his strength as he tried once more. This time Robinson caught him and dragged him up into the forepeak. Beneath them the *Lindeman* was sinking fast. Still gasping for breath, Terjeson was thinking of a way to get them out of the forepeak before it was too late. It was about 4.30 a.m. and still pitch dark. The winds were howling but they had no choice. With their life jackets on, they would take their chances in the water. Terjeson intended to wrench off the forepeak hatch, send the crew out one at a time and follow on last. He struggled with the hatch, trying to force it open against the pressure of the wind. As it burst open, he was sucked by the wind like the cork from a champagne bottle and hurled sideways into the ocean. Water poured into the forepeak and the rest of the crew struggled to get out. The *Lindeman* shifted and groaned as she sank and Robinson, Freeburg, Poole and Newton all burst out of the forepeak. Peter Lenehan was still inside.

Terjeson was hurled against the anchor winch and knocked unconscious. When he came round, he was floating in the water. In the darkness he was unable to see the *Lindeman*, but as he looked around he saw Nigel Robinson floating towards him. The two men grabbed each other. Then they saw Hillary Poole sweeping up on a wave and lunged towards her to grab hold of her. The three hung together in the wild, churning water. They could see no sign of Jeanette Newton, Mark Freeburg or Peter Lenehan. It was still pitch black as they swam and trod water. The winds were still treacherous and the waves were short and strong.

Several metres away Terjeson saw a torch bounce across the water and thought it might be a sign that one of the other crew members was nearby. He called out but the intensity of the wind stifled his cry. He knew the danger of swallowing too much salt water: it would make them drowsy and quickly confuse their thinking. He told the others to keep their mouths shut as the waves washed over them. The wind was making the water choppy, but at least it wasn't too cold. Terjeson felt that if they remained calm there was a good chance they would be found in the water when daylight broke. Together they hung side by side, trying to keep their heads above the turbulent water.

As the night gave way to the first light of morning, it seemed that Cyclone Kathy was moving further towards the mainland coast. The first slivers of dawn light widened and the wind began to ease. Through the foam and spray the devastation of the night could be seen spread across the bays and between the rocks and islands. Eight boats had been dragged up onto the rocks and beaches. Others, though still afloat, had lost their engines or had broken booms. There was no sign of the *Lindeman* or her crew and the message that they were missing was broadcast to the boats still in radio contact.

The call struck a chill in the hearts of the other crews. They knew that the State Emergency Services had been called in but they also knew that the best chance of finding the *Lindeman* crew lay with them. Some of their boats were too badly damaged but those who could get underway would not rest until they had done everything possible to find their colleagues. Water was still coming through the doors and windows of the *Orpheus* but at about 5.00 a.m. Reg Brown told his exhausted crew to pull up the anchors in order to search for the survivors.

By now the wind had dropped to about 40 knots. Brown got a bearing on the island behind him and a radar pitch which told him he had been dragged five nautical miles backwards by the wrath of the storm. As the crew lifted the anchors there was a cry from the mate—in the water right alongside the boat he had spotted the bobbing head of Mark Freeburg. Freeburg was dragged over the side rails and up onto the boat. He had been in the water for a couple of hours and was cold and exhausted. As he explained how they had all shot out of the hatch with the force of the wind and water, Reg Brown radioed the other boats. Just as he finished his call the crew of the *Orpheus* spotted Jeanette Newton in the water a few metres away and dragged her on board. Newton and Freeburg were both shaken and exhausted but uninjured.

Richard Samuels had heard Reg Brown's alarm call. The *Comac Endeavour* had some damage caused by the boom, but was still seaworthy and in better shape than many of the other boats. His decision to move out into the open water had paid off. Although water had burst through windows, doors and hatches and was almost knee height in the wheel-house, Samuels felt that the *Comac Endeavour* had weathered the storm pretty well. He set off to search for the survivors.

Visibility was still poor; the salt spray coming off the waves as they broke was making it harder to see in the full glare of daylight. The *Comac Endeavour* ploughed on through the water, her crew exhausted and drained by their night of terror in the cyclone. The boat combed back and forth as the winds continued to thrash her and the waves and rain filled the boat with more water. The crew strained their eyes as they peered through the fog of rain and spray into the water, hoping to catch sight of a bobbing head or the flash of an orange life jacket.

Chris Terjeson, Hillary Poole and Nigel Robinson had been in the water for several hours. Each time the waves washed over them they closed their mouths and held their breath. They would bob up afterwards, gasping for breath and wondering how much longer they could stay afloat. Their life jackets were waterlogged and heavy and they wondered if they were actually hindering their bid to stay afloat. As the three trod water, with lungs bursting and skin burning from the salt, they saw the *Comac Endeavour*. The boat was obviously searching for them. They raised their arms and waved in the churning water. But their hopes were dashed when the boat turned off in another direction.

As they watched the *Comac Endeavour* growing smaller in the distance, Terjeson knew they must not lose hope. They had to stay calm and hang in there together. The search area was not all that large and he was sure that an aircraft would spot them. They had been in the water for about seven hours, they must just hang on a bit longer. They watched the *Comac Endeavour* moving out until she was about five nautical miles away, and then they saw her coming back towards them. Terjeson struggled out of his orange life jacket and waved it as high as he could reach in the air, hoping that one of the searchers on the boat would see it above the water. This time they had to make sure they were spotted. And they were. The *Comac Endeavour* came up close and the crew threw out the life rings on long ropes to the survivors. Poole and Robinson grabbed the rings and were dragged in while Terjeson swam the last few metres to the boat. As they were dragged up onto the boat, Nigel Robinson looked up at Richard Samuels. 'I knew you'd find me Sam,' he said, grinning at his fellow Kiwi. 'Have you got a beer?'

Robinson, in good shape, was clutching his beer in minutes. Hillary Poole, however, was weak and exhausted and was quickly bundled into one of the crew bunks. Chris Terjeson was cold, exhausted and deeply shaken by the terrifying night. He wanted to rest but was still concerned about his deckhand Peter Lenehan. The search was not over yet.

By now the winds were dropping and the conditions were almost back to normal. A State Emergency Services aircraft was in the air searching and would soon be joined by a KFV plane. The joy of finding five of the survivors was dampened by the absence of the sixth. For as long as the light lasted they searched the bays and inlets, hoping to find their friend and colleague. It was two days later when the body of Peter Lenehan was finally found, floating in the sea near Centre Island. It was never known whether he followed the others out through the hatch or had been trapped inside the *Lindeman*, his body floating out as she sank to the bottom.

The damage Cyclone Kathy caused was extensive. It devastated the small coastal town of Booroloola and left 400 people homeless. The navy had to divert a supply ship to bring food, blankets and other essential provisions to the township. The area's wildlife also suffered. Thousands of white egrets were killed in the mangroves and hundreds of turtles and dugongs had been picked up in the winds and thrown helpless on the salt beds. Wildlife workers and a number of volunteers spent the rest of the week getting the animals back into the water. But Peter Lenehan was the only on to lose his life in the cyclone. KFV Fisheries spent around two and a half million dollars and had staff working around the clock, but they managed to get their boats back in the water in time for the start of the banana prawn fishing season a week later.

For the men and women of the prawn fleet it was a time to celebrate the rescue of the crew of the *Lindeman* and the determination of the crews who set out, after battling all night through the cyclone, to find their colleagues. And it was a time of grieving for the loss of a friend. The crews mourned a good mate, they mourned him knowing only too well that the night of 22 March 1984 was one in which they were all a hair's breadth from disaster during the endless hours that the wrath of Cyclone Kathy wrought havoc in the waters of the Gulf.

A Family Affair

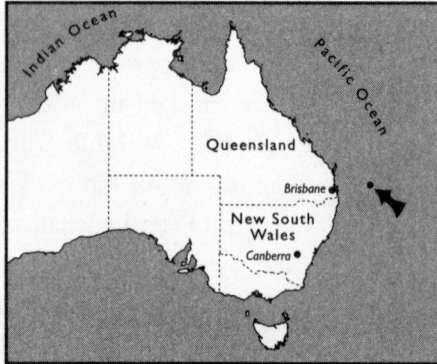

The sinking of the yacht *Tiraumea* off the
coast of Queensland, 26 April 1989.

*'You can call my dad and tell him to come
and get me out of this!'* Bryce Quarrie.

As they worked to keep their sinking yacht afloat, the
Quarries knew they were at the heart of a great adventure. Lashed by a tremendous storm, their world had shrunk
to the tiny, isolated confines of their home, the *Tiraumea*.
Each time the yacht was knocked down under the onslaught
of huge waves, they were thrown about the cabin. Lyn and
Bryce, their seven-month-old son, Stephen and Bryce's 15-
year-old son, Peter, crawled into the tightly packed aft
cabin. They talked about the journey, what had happened,
what they had done and what they might have done differently. They talked about the awesome nature of their present
situation and surprised themselves by being so calm in the
midst of a howling gale and mountainous seas.

Lyn and Bryce Quarrie love the ocean and have spent 13 of their 15 years of marriage on the water. Bryce, who grew up on the north coast of New Zealand, has been sailing since he was eight years old. When Lyn first met Bryce, he was building a boat. She had never been on a boat in her life but she wanted to get to know him, so showed an interest. That interest led to the Quarries living and raising a family on the water and sharing a life-threatening experience.

In 1971 Bryce sailed from New Zealand to Noumea in a Mullet, a shallow draft centre-board boat used for mullet fishing. The boats are popular with fishers in Auckland because they can be easily brought into the harbour and up onto the mudflats, from where it is a quick run to the Auckland fish markets. On the voyage home from Noumea, Bryce and his fellow crewman were hit by a hefty blow 300 nautical miles north of the New Zealand coast. The boat behaved so well in that situation that Bryce knew he wanted to own a centre-board boat.

When Bryce met Lyn in Whyalla, Adelaide, he was building a 13-metre centre-board yacht—an Adams 13, designed by Sydney's Joe Adams. Lyn soon became involved in the building project and her first experience of living on a boat was not on water, but in an industrial yard in Whyalla. For the last 18 months, they lived on board and built the interior around them.

After the *Tiraumea* was finally finished, the Quarries spent more than three years living aboard her in the waters around Whyalla and the Spencer Gulf. In the winter of 1987, Bryce, a lecturer in law, and Lyn, a social worker, gave up their jobs to take a cruise on board the yacht. They explored

the Kangaroo Islands and the ports and coves of the Bass
Strait. Peter went with them, continuing his education
through the South Australian Correspondence School. The
other crew were two cats, Fletcher and Bosun. Life at sea
was cat heaven for them—there were no dogs to chase them
and, apart from keeping dry, all they had to do was repel
invading vermin.

The Quarrie family settled eventually at Lake Macquarie, on the New South Wales coast. In October 1988,
they welcomed a new member to the family—baby Stephen.
Early the following year Bryce was offered a job in Fiji. He
was to lecture in law at the University of the South Pacific.
The Quarries decided to sail to Suva where they would live
on the *Tiraumea* and have a holiday in Noumea en route.
As their home was going with them it wasn't a move requir-
ing packing or selling up, but it did mean a rigorous
program of checking the condition of the *Tiraumea* and a
careful planning of the voyage.

When the Quarries set sail from Newcastle everything
they owned was with them in the *Tiraumea*. They estimated
the trip to Noumea would take between seven and 14 days.
Bryce, Lyn and Peter all shared the duties on the yacht.
Peter had proved himself many times during their previous
sailing trips and the only passengers were baby Stephen,
now seven months old and the two cats. The Quarries were
conservative sailors, meticulous in their planning and preparation, and not the kind to take chances or cut corners.

Studying the winds, they reckoned they would have
about three days' sailing into a headwind. Then the wind
should swing around and they could expect a nice, easy sail

to New Caledonia. But the weather system that delivered that early headwind was based around Tasmania, and instead of moving north, it stalled and stayed there. Each night, Bryce Quarrie was in radio contact with Sydney and Townsville and Penta Comstat, a private marine radio station. Like Bryce, the radio operators were expecting the weather to turn at any time. 'You'll be on your way tomorrow,' they kept assuring him.

Meanwhile, further north, a low pressure cell was developing. The headwinds and conditions down in the Tasman Sea meant that the winds were increasing from the east until they reached 40 to 50 knots. The Quarries were not particularly worried by the conditions, they had sailed through as much and more in the Bass Strait. But they were concerned because this weather had not been predicted and they were not prepared for it.

As the days passed, the easterly winds had built up an easterly swell. When the low pressure system in the north reached the *Tiraumea*'s position, they were hit with strong winds and the winds generated waves from the north. They were caught in a cross action which sent the seas tumbling over each other. The *Tiraumea* rode the conditions surprisingly well, but the force of the wind and water was awesome. Enduring more than 48 hours of heavy weather had put their yacht under extreme pressure. The Quarries battened down and stayed below deck. All they could do was sit tight and hope that no large ship would come along and run into them.

As they sheltered in the main saloon, Lyn and baby Stephen on the leeward side of the boat and Bryce and Peter facing them, they played a tense waiting game. The noise of the storm outside was deafening and the yacht was being tossed around like a matchbox. Each time the massive cross waves hit her, she was thrown up 12 or 15 metres then crashed back down at a terrifying speed. At about 6.30 p.m. Bryce was on the telephone to a friend in Adelaide.

'According to the map, things don't look too good out there ...' his friend commented. At that moment the *Tiraumea* was hit by a huge wave. 'Jeez,' cried Bryce, 'I have to go mate.' And go he did—flying straight through the air to land on top of the stove. Lyn, Stephen and Peter were hurled off their seats and onto the floor. They tried to protect themselves as the cupboard doors burst open and their contents flew around the saloon area. It was the first knock down. The *Tiraumea* crashed over more than 45 degrees, the top of her mast pitching down into the water. As she righted herself the crew staggered to their feet. Stunned by the dramatic hit they looked around them in shock. There was a lot of water in the boat—somewhere there was a hole and they had to find out where.

They discovered a forward hatch had broken and Bryce decided to go outside to try and fix it. The yacht was still pitching wildly, lashed by huge waves and battered by the strong winds. Bryce abandoned his cumbersome life jacket and strapped on two harnesses as he ventured out on deck. The first harness was the short one permanently on the boat. The second harness had a long line of wire rope which Peter, inside the boat, fed out slowly through a slot in the hatch. Peter needed to keep the rope taut so that together he and Lyn had a tight rein on Bryce's movements and, in the case of Bryce falling overboard, they would be able to haul him back to the hatch and then back into the saloon.

As the massive waves crashed over him, Bryce cautiously made his way to the broken hatch. He was able to reach it without incident, repair it and, with Peter drawing the harness rope, make it safely back inside the boat. The *Tiraumea* was watertight again but the weather conditions remained the same, if not worse. The Quarrie family set about making themselves as safe and comfortable as possible inside the boat. They gathered up every cushion, pillow, blanket and soft item on the *Tiraumea* and turned the aft cabin into a padded cell. The knock downs continued, at times as frequently as every ten or 15 minutes. Sometimes there were two king-hits in immediate succession. But still the tough little yacht remained afloat, weathering the massive waves and swell.

As the evening wore on, there was no respite from the weather and no reassurance over the radio that they could expect a break. It was four hours later when the Quarries realised they were taking water again, but this time they couldn't work out where it was entering the boat. They began to pump the water out, Bryce and Peter taking the pump in 15-minute shifts while Lyn stayed with Stephen.

By now Bryce had made contact with the Sea Safety Centre in Canberra. It was after 10.30 p.m. and the *Tiraumea* was 125 nautical miles east off Tweed Heads. Chris Payne, the Sea Safety Centre's Senior Search Coordinator, took Bryce's call over the OTC Maritime Seaphone link. Chris Payne asked Bryce if he wanted to go into full distress mode. This is the decision which all sailors dread and it was

a chilling moment for the Quarries. They had often wondered how they would react in such a situation and now
they knew. They were cool and practical, thinking clearly
and considering every aspect of their situation. There was
no choice but to go to full distress mode and, informing
Chris of their decision, Bryce set off the EPIRB (Emergency
Position Indicating Radio Beacon) and tethered it to the
boat. The Quarries were going to have to abandon ship and
Chris Payne set in motion a major air-sea rescue operation.

The Sea Safety Centre advised the CAA (Civil Aviation
Authority) Rescue Coordination Centres in Brisbane and
then checked AUSREP (Australian Ship Reporting System).
The computer told them that the nearest merchant ship to
the *Tiraumea*'s location was a German container ship, the
Contshipasia. Chris Payne asked the skipper to change
course and head to the scene, hoping the ship would arrive
at about 8.00 a.m. the next morning. Meanwhile the CAA
despatched a twin-winged Beech 200 aircraft to locate the
yacht's emergency beacon. The weather was grim when
pilot Roger Harrison and navigator Tony Snel took off from
Brisbane Airport. They were to fly low over the sea in the
area of the *Tiraumea* but their trip to the area would be a
long one, 150 nautical miles, and they knew it would be
about 3.00 a.m. before they reached the yacht.

While the emergency services snapped into action, the
Quarries continued working to keep their yacht afloat.
They concentrated all of their attention and energy on
baling and pumping and planning the next tasks, but it
was a losing battle. It was about 2.00 a.m. when they
thought they had lost radio contact. Huddling together in

the tiny aft cabin, they reflected on their voyage and the reality of their present situation. They felt as if it was all over but somehow they managed to revive their hope and energy. They began pumping again and the radio crackled back into life. The pump diaphragm broke, but with a knife and a piece of Peter's old wetsuit, Bryce managed to fashion a makeshift diaphragm and get it going again, albeit at only half power.

By 3.00 a.m. Roger Harrison and Tony Snel had sighted the *Tiraumea* and were able to fix her location and report back to the Sea Safety Centre. For the Quarries, the aircraft was a sign that they were no longer alone. The *Tiraumea's* emergency beacon had led the pilots to the correct location but now the yacht was drifting away and the rescue team would not be able to rely on it to fix the yacht's position. They had to maintain a position above the *Tiraumea*, flying dangerously low above huge seas with 45-knot winds gusting at 80 knots. The tiny aircraft was buffeted around and the pilots needed help from the *Tiraumea* to fix her location.

The tremendous noise down on the *Tiraumea* meant that one person was constantly needed by the radio to monitor what was happening. Bryce was on the radio shift talking directly to Tony Snel and Roger Harrison while Peter was fully engaged on the pump. In the chaos of the cabin Lyn rummaged to find a torch. With Stephen strapped to her chest in a baby pouch, she crouched in the companionway, the hatch slightly open, and flashed the torch constantly as a marker for the aircraft overhead. Harrison and Snel could see the yacht below them pitching wildly. At one point when a huge wave hit, they thought the boat and her crew would be lost. 'Can we do anything for you guys down there?' they asked, awed by the crew's situation and their own sense of helplessness. 'Yes,' replied Bryce Quarrie. 'You can call my dad and tell him to come and get me out of this!'

All night the Quarries baled water with plastic buckets and pumped to keep the yacht afloat. Water was cascading down the decks and the waves pounded them continuously. Somehow they kept going. *Contshipasia* loomed towards them in the darkness and stopped a little way off. There was little she could do to help the *Tiraumea* except lie aside to provide protection from the wind. But this would be particularly valuable during any attempt to lift the Quarries off the yacht.

The location of the *Tiraumea* presented real difficulties for the rescue because of her great distance from the coast. The only helicopter which was suitable and available for the job at the time was a Boeing Chinook CH-47C of 12 Squadron RAAF, based at Amberley Air Base, south-west of Brisbane. Piloted by Flight Lieutenant Grant Frost, the chopper took off with a full crew in gale force winds at first light. Also on board was David Parr from the CAA, who would act as dropmaster for the rescue, and the Queensland State Emergency Services' Brett Mitchell, the man charged with the unenviable responsibility of being winched down to the yacht. The Chinook reached the *Tiraumea* at 8.00 a.m. on Wednesday, 26 April, about ten hours after the distress call had been made. The helicopter's range was about 120 nautical miles and it had enough fuel to hold a position above the yacht for about two hours before it had to start the return journey.

By now the Quarries were in direct radio contact with their rescuers. In the lee of the *Contshipasia*, Brett Mitchell began the first of three planned descents to the deck of the *Tiraumea*. Each time, he intended to harness one of the crew and take them back up into the helicopter. To the Quarries, Mitchell looked like Indiana Jones in a fluorescent pink wetsuit. Mitchell himself felt more like a tea bag waiting to be dunked as the strong winds swung him wildly above the yacht. As he drew closer he was buffeted against the *Tiraumea* and had to kick himself off the hull to avoid injury. It soon became clear there was no way he would be able to land on the boat, and Mitchell was winched back up in to the helicopter. The rescue team decided to get the Quarries into life rafts and winch them up into the helicopter from there instead.

The first pair of life rafts was dropped but the down draft from the helicopter drove them away from the yacht. 'Tie a rope to me and I'll go and get them,' cried Peter, who was a strong swimmer. He was soon swimming hard towards the rafts as Bryce let out the rope. But as Peter drew closer to the rafts the rope ran out and he had to swim on untethered through the wild water. Just as he reached one of the rafts and climbed on board, the *Tiraumea* was picked up by a wave and carried closer to the raft. Bryce saw his chance to haul the raft into the yacht.

The Quarries were all wearing life jackets, including Stephen who was then strapped to his father. Bryce quickly unstrapped the baby, strapped him to Lyn and plunged into the water. But before he could swim away from the *Tir-aumea* he became tangled in the rigging and had to struggle for a few precious minutes to free himself. As he broke free, gasping for breath and foundering in the water, he could see the rafts drifting away. He swam on, battling the waves for about 100 metres until he finally reached the raft that Peter was in and clambered into it. The two men were now in comparative safety but they had no way of getting back to Lyn and Stephen on the yacht. Helpless to do anything, Bryce and Peter watched and tried to work out what was in Lyn's mind.

The Quarries were aware that the helicopter only had a limited amount of time to perform three descents. If it took too long the helicopter would reach its final holding time and would have to turn back to refuel. Any delay would jeopardise their chance of being rescued. Bryce and Peter caught sight of Lyn as the *Tiraumea* tossed on the top of a wave the same time their raft rode upward on another wave, then she disappeared out of sight behind a tower of raging water.

The rescue crew dropped a second pair of rafts into the water for Lyn and Stephen. But they landed on the leeward side of the yacht and immediately began to drift away. Lyn took careful stock of her situation. From the moment Bryce had strapped Stephen to her before he leapt off the boat, the baby had stopped moving or making noises. He was wide awake and watching Lyn's face intently as he lay strapped against her chest. Lyn was pretty sure that the second pair of rafts was the last pair that would be dropped. If she was to make it to safety, she would have to take her chance in the water. As the two men had done before her, she jumped into the turbulent water and began a desperate swim through the huge waves to the rafts. As if he understood, Stephen kept still as Lyn swam. If he had wriggled about or struggled Lyn would not have been able to cope in the raging water. Stephen stayed calm and watchful, merely blinking as the water washed over his head.

The rafts had drifted further away from the yacht and Lyn had a desperate struggle to reach them. She was swimming for her life and for Stephen's, and that thought drove her to continue fighting her way against the raging force of the water. Just as she was reaching the limits of her strength, she finally made it to a raft. As she tried to drag herself onto it she froze in terror—she had felt something nudge against her. She had made it to the raft only to have a shark take her. But it was not a shark. It was Brett Mitchell hanging from the helicopter giving her a helping hand from behind! He pushed her up and she somersaulted into the raft. The noise of the ocean and the down draft from the helicopter made it impossible to talk so Brett gestured to Lyn to raise her arms. As she obeyed, he strapped her into the harness and they were winched up out of the raft, swaying wildly in the great gusty winds.

From the other raft Bryce and Peter watched Lyn begin the ascent to the helicopter. Their relief turned to horror when they could not see Stephen. What had happened to the baby? He must have been lost in the water as Lyn was swimming. Bryce knew Lyn was safe and that he and Peter would soon also be in the helicopter, but he was overwhelmed by the loss of little Steve.

Brett Mitchell commenced his second descent, and this time he clasped Peter into the harness but, as they began the lift, Peter became entangled in the drogue lines holding the raft's sea anchor. The flight crew, seeing what was happening, dunked the line holding Mitchell and Peter back into the water. Bryce knew there must be a knife in the raft and he rummaged to find it and then cut the ropes free. Brett Mitchell and Peter began the ascent again with Bryce alone in the raft beneath them, knowing that time was running out. With Peter and Lyn safely in the helicopter it was now Bryce's turn, and he was lifted easily and quickly out of the raft. As he gazed back down at the tumultuous ocean, the great waves breaking and hurling up showers of white spray, Bryce's heart was heavy with thoughts of little Stephen lost somewhere down there in the water.

The noise inside the chopper was tremendous as it wheeled and turned to head back towards the mainland. Lyn and Peter were wrapped in thermal blankets and as Bryce slipped out of the harness, Lyn gave him a beautiful smile. He had expected to see her distraught at the loss of Stephen. Confused, he mouthed 'Steve?' across the chopper cabin. Lyn, still smiling, turned back the corner of her blanket to reveal the peacefully sleeping baby. Bryce couldn't believe his eyes and for an instant thought Stephen must be dead. He struggled across the cabin of the helicopter to touch Stephen to make sure he was alive. 'How is he?' he yelled into Lyn's ear. 'Oh, usual Steve,' she grinned, 'a bath, a feed and a sleep!' As soon as she had reached the safety of the helicopter, she had fed Stephen and he had gone straight to sleep.

The family was together, unhurt and heading for dry land. It was 9.20 a.m. and the Chinook had hovered at the scene for more than an hour and a quarter. It had been a successful operation. Thanks to the superb work of the Sea Safety Centre in Canberra, the Rescue Coordination Centre in Brisbane, RAAF Amberley pilot Grant Frost and the crew of the Chinook, Roger Harrison and Tony Snel in the Beech 200 aircraft, dropmaster David Parr and lineman Brett Mitchell, and the master and crew of *Contshipasia*, four lives had been saved. Grant Frost landed the Chinook at Brisbane at 10.15 a.m.

The Quarrie family had been checked over by medical and nursing officers on the helicopter and there were no apparent injuries. Back on dry land they were whisked off to hospital for a more thorough check. Bryce and Peter were soon released and taken to a motel but Stephen was kept overnight in Brisbane Children's Hospital to make absolutely sure he was none the worse for his amazing adventure. Lyn stayed with him in the hospital.

Lyn, Bryce and Peter had only the clothes they stood up in and a few things given to them by the helicopter crew. Everything they owned, including family heirlooms and personal mementos such as photographs and letters, had gone down with the *Tiraumea*. Apart from their t-shirts and shorts, the only thing they had managed to salvage from the yacht was a knife. It was their only memento. The next morning the Quarrie family prepared to fly out of Brisbane to meet Bryce's family in Auckland. As they went through airport security, the knife set off the alarm, but there was no way they would be parted from their only souvenir.

Barefoot, with no money and no baggage, they stepped out of the airport terminal and onto the Brisbane tarmac.

'Youse can't go out there barefoot,' the security guard warned them. When Bryce replied that they had no shoes, the guard told them to go back into the airport and buy some thongs. 'No money,' Bryce told him. 'Nothing but what we are wearing.' The guard shook his head. 'Youse can't go out there without shoes,' he repeated. 'It's too dangerous!' Bryce, Lyn and Peter laughed at the irony and walked barefoot onto the tarmac to board their flight to New Zealand.

The Quarrie family were filled with gratitude and respect for the skill and courage of the rescue team. Grant Frost, Brett Mitchell and the crew of the Chinook helicopter all received Australia Sea Safety Awards for their heroic and professional rescue. The Quarries were soon inundated with letters and faxes from Australians sending them good wishes and offering clothes, toys and other items to replace all they had lost. As the news of their amazing story spread, more generous offers arrived from a host of other countries and they were overwhelmed by the kindness and generosity shown to them.

Within a few days of arriving in New Zealand, Lyn, Bryce and Peter were looking for another boat. They soon bought a 12-metre yacht but it stayed in New Zealand when the family flew to Fiji four weeks later. They lived for two years on dry land in Fiji but when they returned to New Zealand in 1991, they once again took up life on the water. A few years later they began the task of building another boat, another Adams 13, just like the *Tiraumea*. When they launched it in May 1997, it became their home.

Peter, now a chef, does not live on the boat but still sails. Bryce, Lyn and Stephen love their life on the water as does their new son Sam. The knife is the only memento of their amazing adventure at sea, and of their much loved time on the *Tiraumea*.

'When you have lived through something like this,' says Bryce Quarrie, 'you learn what is important and you know you are among a few people who have been through a most extraordinary adventure.'

A Chance for a New Life

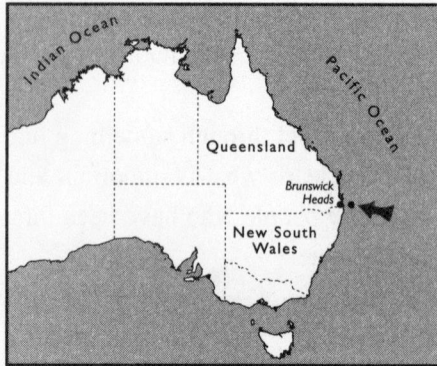

Rescue of the crew from the sinking
catamaran *Moana Ari* off Brunswick Heads,
New South Wales, 9 March 1990.

'Let's take this one wave at a time!' Senior
Constable Eddie Bennet, Gold Coast
Water Police.

Julian Martin was trying to get his life in order. For years
the 32-year-old actor had struggled with a drug habit and
personal problems. The advice of experts in orthodox treat-
ments as well as a range of natural and new age therapists
never quite worked. Even religion, to which he had turned a
couple of years earlier, hadn't helped him confront his
demons. He had become a Christian and although it had
brought moments of peace, the pain and confusion which
had led to his addictive behaviour still raged within. He had
had a troubled childhood, a tormented adolescence and now
he was a man tortured and confused by his past. In 1990, he

had a chance to change his life. With his second wife, Joanna, and his eight-year-old son, Joey, Julian was planning a new life on the water. They gave up their rented house, sold most of their possessions and bought the *Moana Ari*, a 14-metre catamaran which was to be their home at Brunswick Heads on the northern New South Wales coast.

Julian had been sailing all his life. His father, a naval commander, had been a dean of a naval college and as a child Julian had been a sea scout. The *Moana Ari* was his fourth yacht and he was an experienced sailor. Joanna, on the other hand, had never sailed but she was keen to try life on the water with Julian and Joey. The *Moana Ari* was a beauty and they had chosen her because of the spacious accommodation; there was a bridge deck with a big saloon, a main saloon with a forward cabin, a good lounge and three cabins in the hull. She was like a block of flats on water.

The Martins had bought the catamaran from Reg Bladwell, another lifelong sailor who had sailed the *Moana Ari* to the Solomon Islands, the Philippines, and around Australia. As part of the deal Reg, now aged 71, had agreed to sail with Julian from Mooloolaba to Brunswick Heads where Julian would take delivery of the boat. Joanna and Joey were waiting for them in Bangalow.

The two men had a perfect trip as far as Southport where they made a short stop to allow some bad weather to clear. On Wednesday, 7 March they took a look at the weather and decided it was a brilliant day for the run to Brunswick. At about 10.00 a.m. they put out to sea for what looked like a dream sail. It would be a matter of three or four hours at most, so they weren't concerned that the radio was on the blink. In fact, they were so confident of having a short, sweet trip down the home strait that they did not even bother to let anyone know they were leaving.

The weather was beautiful and Julian and Reg made good time until they could see the rock walls of Brunswick Heads about an hour away. It was only then that they saw on the horizon a cyclonic blast, known locally as a 'southerly buster'. This sinister dark grey sky was moving steadily towards them. They immediately switched on the outboard motor and headed for home as fast as possible, but the blast was too quick for them. They were about two nautical miles from the beach when they were hit.

The wind seemed to come from directly above. It had tremendous force which flattened the water and filled it with foam for as far as they could see. The gauge on the *Moana Ari* measured the wind at 75 knots. Almost immediately there was a great crack in the boat and Julian Martin realised that the fore deck of his new yacht was rotten. The boat had been surveyed and passed as sound, but here it was, breaking up before his very eyes. The deck between the hulls just peeled away. There was no time to reduce the sails and as the two men froze in panic, the boat took off like a bat out of hell in the force of the howling winds.

The *Moana Ari* was whipping along at about 20 knots when the anchor broke loose from the cracked fore deck, bounced into the water and hit a piece of plywood sheeting underneath the bridge deck cabin. The plywood hit the outboard and the motor immediately sheared off and was lost. As the two men saw the motor disappear, the sails above them began to shred in the force of the wind. Julian and

Reg were paralysed with fear and it took them almost half an hour to get a grip on their situation and start to move around the boat. By this time the mainsail was completely shredded.

Opting for safety, they hove to and backed the rudder against the jib. Holding head into the wind, they got inside to wait out the blast. But although they waited there was no ease in the weather. In fact, conditions grew worse and as the swell began to increase, a porthole blew out. They knew they were in deep trouble: they had no radio and no one knew they were out there. The waves had become huge and with the floor breaking up beneath them, both hulls were almost a metre deep in water and there was water in the central cabin where they were sheltering.

As the hours ticked endlessly away, there was no relief. The wind and waves continued to pound the boat and the two men were overwhelmed by their situation. They cursed the fact that they had left without advising anyone and that they had left the radio to chance. The only thing to do now was to just keep on waiting in the hope that the weather would change and the boat would hold out. The *Moana Ari* bobbed about on waves towering eight metres high. The two to three metres of breaking white water cresting the waves continually smashed down on the boat. Each time the white water hit the *Moana Ari* she would rear up and something else would break.

On Wednesday night, after more than ten hours of pounding, the two men lay in their bunks and contemplated death. The boat was slowly breaking up around them and several times they were thrown from their bunks and landed in the deep water on the cabin floor. When they hove to they were only a couple of nautical miles from the beach but now they had no idea where they were. They could have been swept miles out to sea or be dangerously close to the beach and rocks.

The night passed with the two men cold, wet and terrified. Dawn brought no relief. The storm continued to engulf them with howling winds and waves that crashed over the boat. Visibility was nil, the noise was deafening and the remaining sail had also shredded to pieces. At about midday, a huge white cap pounded them and Reg Bladwell was thrown from his bunk to the opposite side of the boat, smashing his face and breaking his arm in two places. Julian Martin's terror mounted. Reg was virtually disabled and there was still no sign of relief or reason to hope that anyone would be looking for them. Julian sobbed in terror and then tried to pull himself together by finding some solace in his Bible.

While the two men were sheltering in the cabin of the *Moana Ari*, Joanna Martin was getting worried. She had expected them to sail into Brunswick on Wednesday afternoon. It was now Thursday morning and she had not heard from them. Joanna called Byron Bay Police and reported Julian and the *Moana Ari* as overdue.

The two men on the catamaran were sure they were going to die. There was absolutely nothing they could do to help themselves and the powerlessness they felt added frustration to their fear and panic. In their bunks they lay thinking of their families, contemplating their lives as they faced death in the raging, shark infested waters. Julian

Martin was thinking about his son Joey, who was totally
dependent on him. He was prepared for his own death,
but he believed that Joey would be devastated. The little
boy had only recently recovered from the trauma of his
parents' divorce and Julian could not imagine how he
would cope with the loss of his father. 'If I die,' he
thought, 'Joey will die too.'

Julian clutched his Bible and prayed for Joey. As he
prayed he felt himself being lifted out of his surroundings
and facing a vision of Jesus on the cross, a symbol of the
separation between father and son. It reminded Julian of his
painful childhood discovery, at the age of 11 years, that the
man he thought was his father was not in fact his biological
father. That revelation and the ensuing events had haunted
him ever since. That day on his bunk in the embattled yacht,
Julian had a spiritual experience which took him outside of
his immediate and terrifying surroundings to an oasis of
peace and clarity. At that moment he saw the wound in his
heart and heard the voice of God. He saw the healing hand
of God reach down to him and bind up his heart. The inter-
nal torment which had dogged him for 20 years dissolved
and he knew he was healed. It was a message of love and
hope about Joey too, a spiritual encounter of such impact
that it banished his thoughts of death and drove him up and
out of his bunk in an effort to make it safely back home to
his son.

Julian began to berate Reg Bladwell over the poor safety
provisions on the *Moana Ari*. He was particularly frustrated
that there were no flares on the boat. A tug had passed them
earlier and if they had had flares the tug might have been

able to see them. The two men began to argue. Harsh words were spoken and it was a couple of hours before dark when Reg finally told Julian that the *Moana Ari* did have an electronic position indicating radio beacon (EPIRB) on board. Its batteries were out of date so it was unlikely to work, and in any case Reg didn't want to use it. To set off the beacon would be to jeopardise other lives by attempting a rescue and he was sure they were going to be all right. Julian was not so sure.

Reg believed he was the skipper of the *Moana Ari* and that the decision lay with him. Julian, as the owner of the catamaran believed he had the right to make the decision. He pointed out that Reg was badly injured and that they had no idea where they were. When the storm hit they had been close to the beach. They could easily be driven onto rocks and killed as the boat broke up. Julian was determined to get back to his son. In the end his impassioned pleas won the day.

Although Reg thought it would be a waste of time, they got out the EPIRB. As they set off the beacon Julian's heart was in his mouth. The light went on—it worked! They tied the beacon to a rope, threw it overboard and waited. By now it was late afternoon on Thursday. They had been churning about in the raging water for 30 hours.

At about 4.00 p.m. two aircraft flying over the New South Wales coast picked up the distress tone of a beacon somewhere near Byron Bay. The pilots passed the message to the control tower at Brisbane Airport, who in turn relayed it to the Rescue Coordination Centre (RCC). Duty officers at the RCC contacted the Sea Safety Centre and an RAAF

P3 Orion was sent out to search for the source of the signal. By 7.00 p.m. the Orion had found the *Moana Ari* approximately 23 nautical miles east-north-east of Cape Byron. By now the Gold Coast Water Police and the Gold Coast Helicopter Rescue Service were on the alert. They had matched the EPIRB signal with Joanna Martin's report of the overdue catamaran and knew who and what was in trouble. *Heli 1* from the Gold Coast Helicopter Rescue arrived at the location soon after the Orion.

By this time it was completely dark and violent rain squalls were limiting visibility. The *Heli 1* dropped to a height of about 50 metres above the water and turned its searchlight onto the stricken yacht. Reg and Julian were up on deck, flashing a torch and waving frantically. The moon was blanketed by low cloud and the helicopter was in a violent storm cell with winds raging at 50 knots. Attempting to hold the position was perilous. Although the sails of the *Moana Ari* had been torn to shreds her mast and rigging were still intact and in those conditions a rescue from the deck was impossible. The darkness and the huge swell also ruled out a rescue from the water, as the two men would have been swept away immediately. The helicopter pilot could no longer hold the position above the yacht and turned back to the coast. There was no way the two men could be rescued by air that night.

Back at the Gold Coast Water Police base, Sergeant Peter Stiller, the officer in charge that night, was in contact with the Sea Safety Centre. He had been in touch with police and coast guards at Tweed Heads, Byron Bay and Ballina who reported that big seas were breaking over all bars. Out at Jumpinpin the Southport Air Sea Rescue boat, the *Apex*, had just rescued a small boat which had run out of fuel. The crew of the *Apex* thought the conditions out there were tolerable and this led Stiller to consider the possibility of sending help down the coast, an operation which would take about four hours.

Peter Stiller decided to send out two boats—the *D.W. Wrembeck*, an eight-and-a-half-metre catamaran belonging to the Southport Police, and the *Douglas Cairns*, a 12.5-metre Wright Randell monohull belonging to Harbours and Marine. Greg Turner, the volunteer Air Sea Rescue commander responsible for the *Douglas Cairns* was unable to contact his regular crew so a volunteer crew of three from Air Sea Rescue were appointed to take the boat out. In addition, the Sea Safety Centre had located a 100 000-tonne tanker, the *Ampol Sorel*, and had asked the skipper to divert from his course to the location of the *Moana Ari*. The sea rescue operation had begun.

When the two rescue boats tried to meet up a little later, weather conditions began to deteriorate. On board the *D.W. Wrembeck* Senior Constable Eddie Bennet and Constables Kyle Bates and Neil Paulsen planned to catch up with the *Douglas Cairns* ahead, but had to change course towards Currumbin and then across Kirra Bay to Point Danger. They made good time until they moved out beyond the protection of Point Danger into an area notorious for its wild conditions. The seas that night were up to six metres and the wind between 35 and 40 knots. Both boats were shipping water but they pressed on, hoping for a break in the weather. But there was no break, just more of the same, and the situation started to look hopeless. It was time for the crews to consider their options. They had been informed that the *Ampol Sorel* was heading towards the *Moana Ari* and they considered leaving the rescue to the tanker so they could head back to base.

On the catamaran Reg Bladwell and Julian Martin were still sitting it out. The thrill of seeing the helicopter had subsided and they were once again alone in the dark, cold and huge seas. They had plenty of drinking water on board, but were very hungry. When they left Southport they had only enough food for one meal and that was long gone. A couple of hours after the helicopter had disappeared they saw the huge bulk of an oil tanker coming towards them. At first they thought the *Ampol Sorel* was creating a wind-break to provide protection for a helicopter rescue. But there was no sign of a helicopter.

In comparison to the *Moana Ari*, the tanker looked enormous. Her tanks were empty so she was sitting high in the water, even so the waves were breaking across her decks. The captain of the *Ampol Sorel*, Neil Griffiths, was very familiar with the surrounding waters, but was finding the conditions a challenge. The 100 000-tonne tanker was rolling 30 degrees and Griffiths was having great difficulty controlling her. As the *Ampol Sorel* drew closer to the catamaran, a huge trough developed between the two. The *Moana Ari* was dragged at lightning speed down the steep side of the vast swell and hurled against the tanker's hull. Three times the yacht rose high on the swell and was dragged back down again, crashing into the beam of the tanker. They were tremendous hits which crushed both of the yacht's hulls like concertinas and finally catapulted the catamaran under the tanker's stern at a sharp angle, her propeller lifting high in the air. Julian and Reg hung on for their lives. They felt sure that at any moment they would be crushed between their boat and the tanker or thrown off into the huge surrounding seas.

As the yacht was swept up again on the next swell, the crew on the deck of the tanker threw a rope to the *Moana Ari*. It landed on the deck of the yacht and Julian Martin lunged forward, slipping and sliding as he went, to grab hold of the rope. He immediately wrapped it around the forward beam of the yacht but the hold was brief. As the force of the water drove the yacht away from the tanker, the beam snapped. The *Moana Ari* slid like a matchbox and crashed against the tanker beam again. Overhead, the crew of the *Ampol Sorel* were throwing ladders and ropes, yelling to Reg and Julian to grab them as they snaked down the side of the ship.

The two men could see the *Ampol Sorel* crew waving and gesturing to them, their words lost in the din of the wind and water. To attempt a leap from their yacht to the ropes would mean certain death, they would fall into the raging water or be crushed against the hull of the tanker. A crewman on the *Ampol Sorel* told them through a megaphone that the tanker would try and reposition itself to attempt another rescue. By this stage the *Moana Ari* was semi-submerged. Her deck was at water level with only her cabin above it, and she was constantly being doused by the waves. The tanker started to turn in a wide arc in order to swing back round, a manoeuvre that would take about an hour.

In the distance Julian Martin could see lights. He thought they might be from another helicopter but they soon disappeared and again the two men were left waiting, hoping and praying. The tremendous noise of the wind and water deafened them and they remained wet, cold and terrified. A rescue had seemed within their grasp, but just as quickly it had been ripped away. Now there was only darkness, isolation and the raging storm and sea.

At around 11.30 p.m. the three Water Police on the *D.W. Wrembeck* decided to leave the rescue of the catamaran to the *Ampol Sorel* as the weather conditions had become too dangerous for them to continue any further. The *Douglas Cairns* was in trouble with water in her bilges and had also decided to head back. But just as the two boats were about to abandon the rescue, they received a message from the *Ampol Sorel*. She had collided with the catamaran and damaged it. The *Moana Ari* was taking water even faster and they had not been able to transfer the two crew from the catamaran to the tanker. They would make another try but it would take them some time to complete the manoeuvre.

Eddie Bennet, Kyle Bates and Neil Paulsen looked at each other in desperation. Should they go on and attempt a rescue or should they stick with their much preferred plan of turning back? The *Douglas Cairns* was in some difficulty and although it could risk staying in the area, the crew of the *D.W. Wrembeck* would be on their own as far as the rest of the operation was concerned. The three men talked it over and decided to resume their original course in order to reach the distressed yacht.

As the *D.W. Wrembeck* ploughed through the huge seas, the conditions grew worse. Their speed was down to ten knots. The compass was swinging 30 degrees either side of the course and was virtually useless. The boat had no closed cabin and was taking huge waves over her bow and starboard side. The lights of the *Douglas Cairns* and those on the coast disappeared from sight and Bennet, Bates and Paulsen were in total darkness, navigating only by the moon and stars. Cold and frightened, they wondered whether they would make it to the yacht, whether it was worth the risk of three more lives.

Bennet, at the helm, made radio contact with the *Ampol Sorel* and asked her to put up a flare so they could get an idea if they were still on course. The three men felt a huge surge of excitement as they saw the flare go up. But it soon subsided as they realised that the flare was low on the horizon. This meant they still had a long way to go. About ten minutes later they actually caught sight of the tanker roughly five nautical miles away. It was 1.40 a.m. when they got their next marker from the Gold Coast helicopter. They had another three nautical miles to go. Reaching the limits of their own energy Bennet, Bates and Paulsen constantly talked about giving up. But each time they persuaded themselves and each other to keep going.

They knew that every minute they continued increased the life-threatening risks. Then, when they had already pulled out all stops, the *D.W. Wrembeck* hit a storm cell. The seas were the worst that any of the men had ever seen. The wind increased to 50 knots and the sea rated ten on the Beaufort Scale. The awe-inspiring ferocity of the ocean seemed to envelop them and they thought they would be lost in the waters without ever having reached the yacht. When they were hit by three monstrous waves, Eddie Bennet struggled to hang on to his belief in the boat's ability to make it—he doubted the boat would be able to survive the first wave. The three men were sure they were going to die and had radioed messages of love home to their families. But to their amazement, the *D.W. Wrembeck* surfed over the top of the waves, free-falling into the troughs behind them. In the distance they could see the lights of the tanker. 'Let's take this one wave at a time,' said Bennet, and Paulsen and Bates agreed. They continued to battle the final three nautical miles, one wave at a time, until they could finally see the *Moana Ari*.

Julian Martin could hardly believe his eyes. As he hung onto the cabin pitching wildly at water level, he spotted red and green lights. The lights came and went and Julian wondered what they were. They were too low for a helicopter but too high for a boat. Julian and Reg jumped to their feet and started flashing the torch and shouting. As if by a miracle the little police boat appeared in the gloom.

Eddie Bennet could see that one of the *Moana Ari*'s hulls was completely underwater and that the second was very low. It was hard to make out much in the darkness with only the police boat's light. The helicopter was attempting to hover overhead to provide more light but was not able to hold a position in the fearsome winds. Bennet needed to get the police boat close into the catamaran. But as he attempted it a huge wave quickly swept up behind him and he had to change direction. They began another approach and as they closed in the three police were able to see just how disastrous the situation was.

The *Moana Ari* was breaking up and was surrounded by lumps of wood, ropes and other debris. To get close enough to the yacht the police boat had to risk being hit by the minefield of debris in the water which could fatally foul a propeller. Bennet positioned the police boat six metres upwind of the *Moana Ari*. From the stern of the police boat Paulsen and Bates threw a life ring on a line into the water. Using a megaphone they yelled to the two men on the yacht to jump into it.

Julian Martin and Reg Bladwell were not sure what was happening. The light was so poor and despite the megaphone, they couldn't hear the instructions over the wind. Then, in a thin shaft of light from the tossing helicopter, they saw the ring and Julian heard the voice of one of the Water Police yelling, 'Jump you silly bastards!' Julian and Reg were rocking about on the remains of the yacht. The water looked like a raging morass waiting to swallow them up, but the thought of staying behind was equally terrifying. So they jumped. Reg went first, followed by Julian who was caught momentarily on the rails before falling down into the water. Both men were completely submerged in the water and clutched at each other as they struggled to the surface. Julian wrapped his arm around Reg whose broken arm was hampering his movements, and they caught hold of the life ring.

As the two men were pulled towards the police boat, Bennet realised that to get them aboard the stern he would have to cut the motors or they would hit the propellers. As the ring came closer to the boat Bennet quickly dropped into neutral and yelled to Bates and Paulsen to pull the two men aboard. Reg Bladwell was quickly dragged up but Julian Martin's grip slipped. He dropped back into the water and began to drift away. It was impossible to see beyond the boat and the noise of the wind and water drowned any voices. The Water Police thought they had lost him.

Julian's terror mounted again as he felt his last chance of rescue slipping away. Bennet kept the motors in neutral as the other two strained their eyes through the chaos to spot him. They caught sight of him and threw the life ring out again, yelling to him to grab it. Julian struggled towards the boat and was able to grasp the ring. Just as Bates and Paulsen hauled him up and dragged him on board, a huge wave hit the boat beam on and another one towered and began to break above them. Bennet tried to turn the boat but the wave broke right over them. Both motors were completely covered in water. Neil Paulsen was standing between the motors on the duckboard and was up to his chest in water. Despite being swamped, both engines kept running and Bennet was able to turn the police boat northwards. He wanted to get out of the area as fast as possible, fearing a collision with the wrecked yacht.

Julian Martin and Reg Bladwell were wrapped in blankets in the aft of the police boat. 'Thank God we're safe,' Martin said. 'We don't know if we're safe yet,' one of the rescuers replied. It would take them at least three hours to make the trip back to Southport and they were very low on fuel. Bennet, Bates and Paulsen were also suffering from cold and exhaustion, but it was crucial to act immediately and get away from the area and to slightly safer conditions.

The run back to Southport was risky and arduous. Bennet got a compass course from Peter Stiller back at headquarters to help him navigate. The sea conditions were confusing, with no consistency to the waves or swell. Each wave had to be felt out and negotiated individually and intense concentration and highly skilled seamanship was required to keep the boat square. The big seas lifted the *D.W. Wrembeck* up and sent it surfing down eight- and ten-metre waves, and each time she risked capsizing.

By 2.30 a.m. the *D.W. Wrembeck* was dangerously close to running out of fuel. Even though she was reaching the limits of her capacity, Eddie Bennet managed to keep her going, running ahead of some waves while dropping back on others, then trying to outrun the one behind. It took about half an hour to get clear of the storm cell and into slightly better weather conditions. Although there was some moonlight to lift the intensity of the darkness, they still could not see the lights on the coast and had great difficulty in getting a fix on their position. For a while the helicopter was monitoring them from above but it too was low on fuel, and had to leave the area. The boat was once again alone on the seas.

At 4.30 a.m. the *D.W. Wrembeck* radioed that she was out of fuel on one tank but could see the lights of Bayview Harbour. Twenty minutes later the other tank was empty. The boat was now about nine nautical miles east of Surfers Paradise. An hour later the Volunteer Coast Guards reached them and refuelled the police boat. It was 6.15 a.m. when the *D.W. Wrembeck* made it back to Southport. Her crew were cold and exhausted and had sore and strained muscles.

Reg Bladwell and Julian Martin were taken to hospital where Reg's broken arm was set and Julian was treated for broken ribs.

The following day a marine salvage team set out to find the *Moana Ari* and reported that her centre cabin and decks had been washed off the semi-submerged hulls. The salvage team's intention had been to dive and take a look to see whether the boat could be saved. But the area was alive with sharks and the task was abandoned. Instead, orders were given for a tanker in the area to ram the *Moana Ari* and break her up to prevent her from becoming a shipping hazard.

There is no doubt that if the three Water Police had abandoned the search and turned back to land, Julian Martin and Reg Bladwell would have been washed from the remains of the *Moana Ari* and lost at sea. It took outstanding courage and skilled seamanship to get the small open police boat through such extraordinarily hazardous conditions. On numerous occasions the Water Police had felt like turning back. But they continued on, taking it one wave at a time through the storm cell to rescue the two men and then made the long and dangerous journey home. Senior Constable Eddie Bennet had skippered the boat with Constable Neil Paulsen handling communications. Constable Kyle Bates, who at the time had only been with the Water Police for six months, acted as deckhand and assisted with the job of hauling the men on board. The three received Sea Safety Awards. Commendations also went to the volunteer Air Sea Rescue crew in the *Douglas Cairns* which had been standing by to assist and support the *D.W. Wrembeck*.

Julian Martin and Reg Bladwell had faced death and been given another chance at life. With the insurance money from the wrecked yacht, the Martins bought a ketch and set up home on it, just as they had planned to do with the *Moana Ari*. But for Julian Martin the ocean had lost its appeal. Each time he sailed memories of his devastating ordeal in the *Moana Ari* would return. The Martins lived on the boat for nine months, then swapped their boat for a house on land.

For Julian Martin, the rescue was more than just a spectacular escape from the jaws of death. The spiritual encounter he experienced as he lay in his bunk in the stricken yacht changed the course of his life. Since his vision that day, he stopped using drugs and has been free of the torturous confusion and pain that had been driving his addiction. Seven years later Julian believes he is a living testimony to the existence of God and is actively involved in church life. He now spends a lot of time talking with church groups and other community groups about his experiences, his encounter with God and his subsequent rescue from death on the formidable waters off Australia's eastern coast.

Falling From the Sky

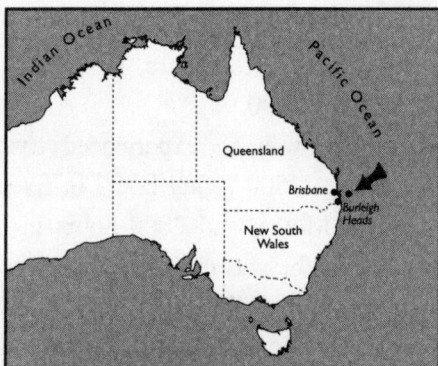

A Hot-air Balloon Rescue off the Gold Coast,
2 October 1990.

'I nearly organised my own funeral!' Funeral
director Alex Steel, passenger in the hot-air
balloon.

Balloonists will tell you that ballooning is the safest way
to fly and all the evidence suggests this statement is
correct. But it will take a lot more than that to convince
Sylvia Steel and Judith Goodwin, two Sydney women who
almost lost their lives in a ballooning accident. Freak winds
turned a pleasure flight into a nightmare for the women and
for Sylvia Steel's husband, Alex. And it virtually grounded
the reputation of Australia's ballooning pioneer, Roger
Meadmore.

At the age of 61, Alex Steel was something of a daredevil. He loved trying new things and had developed a taste
for adventure sports. Whitewater rafting, abseiling, gliding

and rock climbing—he had tried them all. Next on the agenda was a ride in a hot-air balloon. He booked himself a flight with Lovely Champagne Balloon Flights and was to meet his pilot, Roger Meadmore, for an early morning take-off on 2 October 1990.

Roger Meadmore was an experienced flyer. He had clocked up more than 1500 flying hours in fixed wing aircraft, mainly Tiger Moths, and 2000 hours in balloons in six countries. In 1990 he was the most experienced balloon pilot in Australia. In 1983, the same week that Alan Bond snared the America's Cup for Australia, Meadmore won the World Ballooning Championship in Nantes, France, with Peter Vizard. Meadmore loved flying balloons. He loved the peace and silence, the sense of floating like a free spirit above trees and fields, and the ability to fly very slowly, almost at walking speed, quite low over the ground. He had been the first person in Australia with a balloon and had operated a highly successful charter flight business in Brisbane, taking Expo visitors on stunning trips across the city. In October 1990, he was operating a leisure flying business and also owned a number of pancake restaurants around Australia.

Sylvia Steel got up at the crack of dawn to drive her husband to meet up with Roger Meadmore. Sylvia hated heights and while she was happy for her husband to fly, she had no intention of being in that basket when it left the ground. The balloon flight that morning was to have another passenger on board, Judith Goodwin, a Sydney librarian. Like Alex's wife, Judith's husband had no desire to try ballooning so she was taking the flight by herself. The Steels gave her a lift to the meeting with Meadmore at one of his pancake restaurants, and from there they all drove to Nerang for the launch.

The balloon was in a trailer on the back of Meadmore's four-wheel drive. The sky was a little overcast that morning and this meant that the passengers wouldn't be able to take the most spectacular of photographs. But despite this, Meadmore assured his passengers that they would get some terrific views. The forecast that morning was calm—no winds on the ground and four knots (about walking speed) at 150 metres. Those conditions would take them in a southerly direction towards Coolangatta Airport. When the group arrived at the launching ground, Meadmore checked the wind by sending up a test balloon. The small helium balloon shot upwards and floated away on the wind.

The Steels and Judith Goodwin helped to unload the balloon from the trailer. Taking this great mass of nylon fabric and spreading it out on the ground in preparation for it to be attached to the basket, added to the general air of excitement and sense of adventure. The balloon, a Cameron 105, was a pale silvery blue with the trademark of the pancake restaurants—the face of a young woman with flowing hair—printed on it in deep maroon.

Once the basket was attached to the fabric, the next task was to connect two LPG tanks into the balloon's burners. When they were switched on, a great rush of blue flames leapt out of the burner and ignited the gas. Alex Steel and Judith Goodwin held the balloon open while Roger Meadmore carefully controlled the flow of the flame up into the swelling mushroom of the fabric. It took about 15 minutes to fully inflate the craft. The balloon had reached the height of a nine-storey building and was straining at the anchor ropes, ready to lift at any moment. She seemed sturdy but elegant, possessing all the magic and mystery that has captured the imagination of storytellers since ballooning first began.

Alex Steel couldn't wait to get going and was itching to climb into the basket. One thing that would make the experience perfect for him would be if Sylvia joined him. The preparations had been very exciting and Sylvia was getting some niggling second thoughts on the idea. Alex and Judith were already on board and as Roger Meadmore climbed in alongside them he looked back to Sylvia and asked her if she was quite sure she didn't want to join them. In a change of heart, Sylvia hurled caution to the wind and scrambled into the basket. The pilot and his other two passengers were delighted. Alex Steel was especially thrilled to be able to share his adventure with his wife. It was just after 6.00 a.m. when Meadmore completed his checks of the balloon, notified the control tower of his intention to take off and was given airway clearance. The anchor ropes were released and they were airborne and climbing rapidly.

The wind was more than Meadmore had expected and certainly more than the forecast had indicated. At take-off there had been a pleasant north-westerly wind. But now, instead of heading south they were being blown to the east. Meadmore was sure that once they got a bit higher they would be above the wind and he would be able to correct his position. He radioed Coolangatta control tower again and requested permission to rise to 1520 metres. This would take him well above the ground current and out of the force of the westerly wind.

Clearance immediately came back from the tower and Meadmore took the balloon higher. As they lifted above 1220 metres, he grew uncomfortable with the wind. It was clearly not a ground current and he wasn't going to be able to rise above it to get free. The passengers sensed some tension in their pilot. But apart from thinking that they were travelling a little faster than anticipated, they were not too concerned. By now Meadmore's instruments were telling him that they were travelling at 30 knots. Things were getting out of hand and the balloon would soon be over water. Meadmore knew it was time to make a decision. He decided to abort the flight and discharged some air from the top of the balloon by tugging on the air release lanyard. This took the balloon into a rapid descent. Meadmore radioed the control tower at Coolangatta once again and told them that he planned to take the balloon down to a landing on the beach.

As they saw the ground rushing up to meet them, the slight concern that Judith Goodwin and Alex and Sylvia Steel were feeling quickly turned to stark fear. Meadmore was planning to collapse the balloon when the basket touched down, but as the balloon plummeted he realised they were descending too fast. To land at that speed would be fatal. He was going to have to keep flying and that meant flying out over the sea. He instantly radioed a mayday to Coolangatta. 'We're not going to make the beach,' he told the tower. 'Call Air Sea Rescue!' The tower told Meadmore to keep flying and that help would be on its way.

Meadmore steadied the balloon and attempted to reassure his passengers. It was a nasty situation and he could sense their mounting fear. He explained to them that he would have to land in the ocean but would not do so until help was standing by in the water below. He would keep flying until the rescue boats caught up with them, then he would safely take the balloon down into the water and they would be picked up by the boats. There was no danger, he said, but they were going to have a wet end to their flight.

Meadmore was a lot more concerned than he sounded. He had enough gas to keep going for one and a quarter hours. After that he would have no alternative but to ditch the balloon in the sea—regardless of whether there was a rescue boat nearby. With no life jackets this could be fatal. But the tower had said rescue boats were on the way, so there was every reason to assume that they would arrive at the balloon's location in time.

The weather was getting worse. The balloon kept moving into great patches of icy mist which seemed to wrap around them and envelop the whole balloon. When the Steels and Judith Goodwin got a glimpse of the water below they were horrified. The waves seemed enormous. However would they survive a ditching in the sea? The three passengers were feeling real terror. Judith was sure she was going to die on this day of all days, her daughter's birthday. Sylvia Steel was holding tightly onto her husband's hand. She was inwardly cursing her decision to join the flight but was also thankful that they were experiencing this ordeal together. Alex Steel was keen on adventure but this was proving to be a bit too much for him. The balloon continued moving rapidly out to sea and there was no sign of a rescue boat.

Constable Greg St Clair of the Gold Coast Water Police was woken up by a telephone call informing him of the balloon's plight. Within minutes he was dressed, out of his house and on his way to Water Police Headquarters, north of Surfers Paradise. On arrival there, he took control of the *D.W. Wrembeck*, the eight-and-a-half-metre catamaran which had been used by his colleagues some six months earlier to rescue the sinking *Moana Ari*.

Sergeant Neville Cooper was already on board the *D.W. Wrembeck*, and the two men were soon heading out in the direction of the balloon. They knew they didn't have much time and that they had to travel faster than the wind if they were to catch up with the balloon. To make matters more difficult, the sea was getting stronger and the waves had increased to about two metres. St Clair had to take great care to prevent the boat from riding the waves too fast. It would be easy for the police boat to pitch forward and then they would take on water. This would slow them down and could swamp the engines. Ahead of the *D.W. Wrembeck* was the *Apex II*, a twin-hulled boat from the Southport Air Sea Rescue, skippered by volunteer Greg Turner.

The tension in the balloon was mounting. Coolangatta tower had advised Roger Meadmore that help was on the way, but so far there was no boat to be seen and there was only ten minutes' worth of fuel left. The balloon was still travelling fast and Meadmore knew that any rescue boat would have its work cut out trying to catch up with them.

Meadmore had landed a balloon on the back of a boat

before, but that was 15 years ago and the weather conditions had been extremely calm. It seemed he might have to try a similar manoeuvre this time. His passengers were obviously very frightened and he wasn't sure how they would cope with the ocean or a boat landing. He saw the two little rescue boats cutting through the rising waves and moving fast towards them, and thought that an attempt to land on one was now a real possibility. It might prove safer than landing in the water where the basket would be immediately swamped.

Cooper and St Clair in the *D.W. Wrembeck* and Greg Turner and his colleagues in the *Apex II* had spotted the balloon and made good speed towards her. As they neared the location they could see Meadmore gesturing from the basket. He seemed to be indicating that he would attempt a landing on the deck of the *Apex II*. As Meadmore allowed the balloon to sink down gently, Greg Turner attempted to keep his boat travelling at a steady, consistent speed to enable Meadmore to bring it in comfortably. But neither skipper nor pilot could have anticipated the huge wave which suddenly knocked the boat sideways and out of the balloon's line of descent. The basket was almost touching the water but quick as lightning Meadmore primed the gas and the balloon lifted to a safer position. Turner swung the boat around to get back into position. But as Meadmore brought the balloon in, the boat was knocked by the swell and reared up, smashing into the balloon's basket.

The boat and the basket met with terrifying force. The passengers clung to the rails and to each other as the basket tipped onto its side with a huge jolt and a deafening noise. As it hit the water, the wind caught the fabric of the balloon and whipped it up like a spinnaker carrying the basket behind in the water at about 15 knots.

Roger Meadmore, Judith Goodwin and Alex and Judith Steel were tossed around mercilessly as the basket bounded over the swell. The icy water washed over them with such force that they were pinned to the sides of the basket as if they were on a fairground ride. Wave after wave swamped them and they struggled to get their heads above water. They thought they would be trapped in the basket and struggled desperately to free themselves. With a huge surge of energy, Sylvia Steel pulled on the balloon wires and hoisted herself up out of the basket and jumped. She sank deep into the churning water and thought her lungs would burst as she struggled to get back up to the surface. She thought she had freed herself, but to her horror something was holding her back. As she had taken off over the side of the basket, a rope from the balloon had wrapped around her ankles, and the movement of the balloon and her struggle had tightened it. Now it was pulling her down under the surface as the balloon scudded along on top of the water.

On the *D.W. Wrembeck*, Greg St Clair had watched in amazement as the balloon made its two landing attempts, then ditched in the water. He kept his eyes on the basket to try and assess what the passengers and pilot would do. Then he saw Sylvia Steel go over the side. He thought he would be able to pull her out of the water as soon as she surfaced. But as he waited, there was no sign of her bobbing head in the water. The seconds ticked away until almost a minute had passed. St Clair was sure something must be holding Sylvia under the water otherwise she would have resurfaced by now. He narrowed his eyes and focused intently on the surface of the water, searching for some sign of her. Then he saw it—some fabric under the water. In an instant he was over the guard rail of the boat and in the water beside her. Sylvia was kicking madly in an attempt to free her leg from the rope. St Clair's hand sought out the rope and followed it by touch until it led him to the loop which was caught around her foot. He wrenched the rope away from Sylvia and she bounced up to the surface. Gasping for breath, she was hauled aboard the *D.W. Wrembeck* by Neville Cooper. As Sylvia was thanking her rescuers she could see her husband and Judith Goodwin being dragged out of the rapidly sinking balloon basket and into the safety of the *Apex II*. Relieved, she sank back onto the deck.

Roger Meadmore was the last to struggle onto the police boat. He had always brought his passengers home safely and he had feared that this might be his first fatality. Shaking with cold but enormously relieved, he and Greg St Clair set to work on salvaging the balloon. They had to cut more than 15 holes in the fabric to drag it in from the water. Back on land, it was hosed down and cleaned before work could begin on the repairs.

The balloon's three passengers were soon back on dry land and very much aware of their lucky escape. Alex Steel had hurt his shoulder while struggling in the basket, but otherwise the passengers had no injuries from their encounter with the ocean. The speed and efficiency with which the boat crews reached them had been the difference between life and death, and the courageous action of Constable Greg St Clair had saved Sylvia Steel from drowning.

The balloon had drifted 15 nautical miles off the coast before its pilot had been able to bring her down. Roger Meadmore was widely criticised for his decision to take off that morning in such strong north-westerly winds, but the forecast had been misleading. 'I admit I misread the weather that morning,' Roger Meadmore says. In retrospect, he sees that he could have taken different action to prevent his passengers from becoming trapped in the basket or swamped by the balloon. They could have jumped from the basket into the water before it ditched. But it's always easy to be wise after the event. Roger Meadmore was more experienced than any other balloon pilot in Australia, but since the accident his ballooning career has virtually ground to a halt. Damage to the balloon was estimated at around $15 000 and there was the additional loss of several thousand dollars' worth of radio equipment.

As a result of the rescue, Constable Greg St Clair of the Gold Coast Water Police was awarded a Queensland Police Service Commissioner's Certificate for initiative, resourcefulness and dedication to duty. Sylvia Steel was amazed to find that her crippling fear of heights had disappeared, and Judith Goodwin was able to celebrate her daughter's birthday and look forward to the next one. As for Alex Steel, his first balloon flight remains a vivid memory. From the safety of dry land the Sydney funeral director joked, 'I nearly organised my own funeral!'

Averting an Environmental Disaster

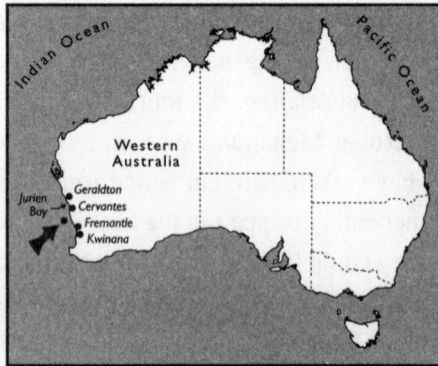

Rescue from the *Kirki* oil tanker off the coast
of Cervantes, Western Australia,
21 July 1991.

*'If we hadn't saved the thing my name would
have been mud, I reckon,'* Rolf Farstad,
skipper of the rig tender *Lady Kathleen.*

The story of the *Kirki* is more than just the rescue of 37
lives from a stricken oil tanker. It is a story of how a
crippled ship became a floating disaster area, threatening
marine life, wildlife, and the livelihoods of cray fishermen
and nearby coastal communities, and of how salvage
workers risked their lives to avert what could have become
Australia's worst environmental maritime disaster.

The *Kirki* was built in Spain in 1969. She had sailed
under many different flags before being bought by the Kirki
Shipping Corporation SA of Liberia in 1986, to be managed
by Mayamar Marine Enterprises of Piraeus, Greece. The

story begins in June 1991 when the *Kirki* arrived in the Gulf of Oman on the east coast of the United Arab Emirates. She had come from Yanbu on the Red Sea carrying a cargo of fuel oil. The fuel oil was transferred to another ship and the *Kirki* sat at anchor off Fujairah. Fifteen days later, she headed on to Jenel Dhanna in the Arabian Gulf to load a cargo of light crude oil. The crude was destined for the BP refinery at Kwinana, Western Australia. During her stay in the Gulf of Oman no record of maintenance or any other work being carried out was entered in the ship's logs.

The oil tanker set out for Kwinana under the command of Captain Eleftherios Efstathopolous, an experienced seafarer with 22 years at sea, 20 of which were on tankers. The *Kirki* called back briefly at Fujairah to drop off five crew members and pick up a second mate. When she sailed from Fujairah on 3 July, there were 35 crew and two crew members' wives on board. As the *Kirki* sailed through the Gulf of Oman, the weather was fair. But once past the protection of the Arabian Peninsula, the crew began to feel the effects of a south-west monsoon. For a few days the weather was stormy, sometimes with 35- to 40-knot winds and four-metre swells.

Ships approaching Australian waters enter the AUSREP (Australian Ship Reporting) area, and are under the auspices of the Canberra-based Australian Maritime Safety Authority (AMSA). The *Kirki* entered AUSREP on 11 July and from then on reported daily to the Rescue Coordination Centre. Her estimated time of arrival at Kwinana was 11.00 p.m. on 20 July.

As the *Kirki* approached the Australian coast, the

weather took a turn for the worse. A low pressure cell began to move south-east, its course running parallel with that of the ship as she travelled southwards about 200 kilometres from Carnarvon. This area is a jewel in a magnificent stretch of coast. At Shark Bay the Dutch seafarer Dirk Hartog landed in 1616, and close by in the gentle waters of Denham Sound, the famous dolphins of Monkey Mia frolic in the shallows alongside humans.

As the ship continued on towards Geraldton, passing the Abrolhos Islands, her route and speed were normal. The weather grew worse and strong winds and high seas began to lash and rock the tanker. Captain Efstathopolous slowed her and revised the estimated arrival time. The *Kirki* was now expected to reach Kwinana at 9.00 a.m. on Sunday, 21 July. But she would never make it.

In the early evening of Saturday, 20 July the weather started to deteriorate. As force eight winds howled outside, the engineer in charge noticed a change in the fuel load gauge. It warned him that the main engine was under a heavy load. He reported it to the chief engineer, Nikolas Bijarakis, who checked that the cylinders were all working and then reported the situation to the captain. By 8.00 p.m. the ship's speed had to be reduced and a course alteration made to cope with the worsening weather conditions. The *Kirki* was sluggish and took around 20 minutes to complete the course alteration of just 45 degrees. She was also showing a trim to the bow.

Captain Efstathopolous became uneasy. His ship was struggling and he could not pinpoint the cause. He sent the chief mate and five other crewmen to check out the bow space. To make it along the deck to the forecastle was a dangerous task and required extreme caution. Heavy seas were breaking over the decks, rain was lashing the ship and the gale-force winds could easily sweep the men away. Efstathopolous slowed the *Kirki*'s speed to reduce the heavy seas breaking over the ship. As the men opened the weather-tight doors locking off the forecastle, a great rush of wind swept out of the locked space and air could be heard swishing through the vents.

The men had been joined by the chief engineer, Bijarakis and were shocked to discover that the forepeak was fast filling with water which had reached sea level. The bad news was promptly passed to the bridge and once again the captain slowed down the *Kirki*'s speed. The crew set up the ballast pump to get rid of the water, but it made no impression on the water level. Somehow that section of the ship was open to the sea and water was continuing to pour in faster than the ballast pump could pump it out. The captain decided to reduce the severe trim in the ship's bow by transferring some of the cargo to another cargo tank which had spare capacity. The pumps were started and the operation took about three quarters of an hour. By 2.00 a.m. the operation was complete and the *Kirki* was about 16 nautical miles from the coast.

The weather conditions seemed to be worsening by the minute. Heavy seas broke over the deck as the ship rolled and yawed in force eight winds. Her speed was now down to less than three knots. Up on the bridge, Captain Efstathopolous, the chief engineer Bijarakis and the second mate surveyed the overcast sky and the churning waters buffeting their ship. It was just after 2.00 a.m. They knew they had a problem but were unable to identify its nature or the cause of the water flowing into the forward section. They were thankful that they were not far from Fremantle.

As the three men gazed along the length of the ship, they twice saw the light on the *Kirki*'s foremast seemingly bend towards the bridge, then straighten. As the light bent for the third time, they watched amazed as the foremast and the forepeak of their vessel disappeared below the waves. Immediately fire broke out in the forward section, and the officers and crew were transfixed with horror as huge flames leapt upwards. The *Kirki*, with her huge and highly volatile cargo of crude oil, was ablaze and her bow had broken away, disappearing into the pitch black depths of the ocean.

Almost as fast as it had started, the fire was flooded by seawater and extinguished. But it was followed by a second blaze as oil gushing from the cargo tank ignited. Captain Efstathopolous ordered a mayday call but it was broadcast on a VHF short range channel and there were no other vessels within range at the time. Forty minutes later, at about 3.00 a.m., the mayday signal was sent again by medium frequency telephone and two-tone alarm. It was picked up by Perth Radio, Sydney, Darwin, Townsville and Singapore. But none of those stations could make return radio contact with the *Kirki* and the radio officer who transmitted the message had failed to give any information on the ship's condition or even state her position.

Fortunately, staff at Perth Radio remembered that Efstathopolous had made a call to Fremantle by radio telephone earlier in the night. The skipper had called Captain

Above 18. The airlift from the Greek oil tanker, *Kirki*.
Overleaf 19. The *Kirki*'s bow broke off amidst balls of fire.

20. Isabelle Autissier waiting to be rescued from her yacht, *Ecureuil*.

21. The Seahawk helicopter winches a rescuer down to Isabelle Autissier.

22. Isabelle Autissier faces a press conference after her successful rescue.

23. Raphael Dinelli waves to the aircraft crew as his yacht, *Algimouss*, sinks.

Above 24. Tony Bullimore swims out from the *Global Exide Challenger*.

Overleaf 25. Orion Rescue 253 tell Thierry Dubois that help is coming.

EXPECT RESCUE
IN 48 hrs
BY HMAS
ADELAIDE
(HELICOPTER)

Chandras, the port captain from Mayamar Marine Enterprises, the company that managed the *Kirki*. Chandras had arrived in Fremantle to meet the ship. Radio operators checked back on the numbers and managed to contact Chandras who was able to give them an approximate position for the ship. With this information the Rescue Coordination Centre (RCC) and the Civil Aviation Authority (CAA) Rescue Coordination Centre in Perth triggered the procedure for a helicopter rescue.

The lack of information in the ship's mayday call hampered the rescue services' preparations. They didn't know what to expect and certainly had no indication of the potential for large scale pollution. Back on board the *Kirki*, a third fire had broken out and this time it took more than the action of the ocean to douse it. The flames ignited the leaking oil which was floating on the surface of the water. Driven by the strong winds, the fire licked down the side of ship and looked set to engulf the section housing the crew's cabins. The risk of the fire sweeping across the deck was imminent. If it was not stopped it could ignite the remaining cargo tanks full of crude oil and turn the *Kirki* into a floating furnace. In a frantic effort the crew used water cannons to flood down the side of the ship. They were attempting to create a barrier of water in order to protect those vital areas and contain the fire.

Overhead, a Qantas Boeing 747 caught sight of the burning ship through the fog. Flight QF8 had been heading into Perth but had been asked to divert from its route by Perth Rescue Coordination Centre. The pilot reported that the fire was so large and intense he thought the ship must have been destroyed. But again, nature intervened and the third fire was eventually doused by seawater.

The risk of further fires remained. In the darkness the tanker was rolling heavily and the crew and passengers were terrified. Their sense of isolation was overwhelming. Because fires were breaking out everywhere there was no place on the ship which could be considered safe. At any time burning oil could break onto the decks and turn the tanker into a furnace.

Efstathopolous's responsibility was to protect the lives of his passengers and crew. He ordered the ship to be stopped and mustered the crew in readiness to abandon ship. The *Kirki* pitched and rolled through the fog as the waves towered above her and crashed across the deck. The crew had assembled on the leeward side of the ship and struggled to lower the port lifeboat and life raft. But it was futile in the face of the huge swell and gale force winds. The lifeboat rocked perilously and it was clear there was no way it could be launched safely. As they attempted to winch it back up towards the deck, the lifeboat crashed several times against the ship's side and became entangled in its own wires and rope ladder. Struggling to lock the boat back in position, the crew were horrified as more fires erupted.

The RCC relayed the *Kirki*'s mayday call to an oil rig tender, the *Lady Kathleen*, situated about 90 nautical miles away off Rottnest Island. Just after 4.30 a.m. she set off at full steam to assist the *Kirki*. Around the same time the Department of Marine and Harbour's vessel, the *Vigilant*, also set a course for the *Kirki* from Fremantle harbour.

Captain Efstathopolous was concerned about the shallow water and sandbars which were now only a few kilometres east of the *Kirki*'s position. He ordered a change of position in the hope of keeping the tanker away from the coast. With a great roar, a fifth fire of intense ferocity erupted. Its massive flames snaked upwards and its light and heat terrified the crew. It looked as though this blaze would engulf the *Kirki*, but once again, the ocean doused the fire. Like a cat, the ship seemed to have nine lives, although to the crew it seemed they were rapidly running out.

Three hours after the *Kirki*'s bow had broken, Perth Radio was finally able to make contact with the ship. A helicopter would not be able to land on the tanker's deck but it could winch the crew to safety. Communications were complicated by language difficulties, but the message was finally understood. The captain of the *Lady Kathleen*, Rolf Farstad, was also able to get through to the *Kirki* by radio and let Efstathopolous know that he too was on the way. The helicopters were delayed by heavy fog and Captain Farstad radioed the *Kirki* again and explained the delay. He assured Efstathopolous that the *Lady Kathleen* would rescue his crew from the water or another means of rescue would be found.

The RAAF and Police Airwing crews took off around 6.30 a.m. in conditions that would have deterred many others. There was thick fog, just six metres of visibility and gale force winds, but they battled on to reach the *Kirki* and begin the long and dangerous rescue operation.

The RAAF helicopter was the first to reach the *Kirki*, followed by the police chopper minutes later. Nikolas

Bijarakis on the *Kirki* was experienced in air–sea rescues and as the two helicopters hovered about 15 metres above the ship, he helped the rescuers get the crew members into the safety harnesses. Every moment of the operation was fraught with danger. Driving rain reduced visibility to a minimum and the rescuers were buffeted by gale force winds. Beneath them, the *Kirki*, still throwing up sudden fires, thrashed about in the wild seas, lashed by five-metre waves which broke over her deck.

Around 7.15 a.m. the first of the crew were winched into the safety of the helicopter. As they rose in the air, the roll of the ship sent them flying out five metres either side of the ship. On more than one occasion, it looked as though lives might be lost in the rescue. One man threw his hands up to his face only a few metres from the helicopter and almost slipped from the harness. For tense moments, the Police Airwing's Senior Constable Ray Rudge, who was hanging out of the helicopter to winch him aboard, thought the man was lost. No one could survive a fall in the turbulent seas below. But the man hung onto the harness and made it into the safety of the helicopter.

The rescue was a death-defying operation in which the helicopter crews risked everything and brought all their skill and fortitude to bear in extraordinarily dangerous conditions. The weather conditions alone were extremely dangerous for a small helicopter holding a position at a low level, but coupled with the status of the ship, the situation was life-threatening. At any time the tanker was likely to erupt in flames, which would instantly and fatally ignite the helicopters. One by one, the rescuers lifted every passenger, officer and crew member off the *Kirki* and shuttled them to Cervantes and Jurien Bay in a four-hour operation.

One of the rescue helicopter pilots had reported to the CAA in Perth that the *Kirki*'s bow had broken and that oil was leaking from the ship into the water. This information was passed onto the RCC who asked Captain Farstad on the *Lady Kathleen* to assess the situation when he arrived at the scene. In the meantime, plans were being made to attempt a salvage operation. The Marine Pollution Section of the Australian Maritime Safety Authority (AMSA) contacted Ken Ross, the Managing Director of United Salvage, the only Australian company with the resources to undertake a major salvage operation at such short notice. Ross was soon in contact with the owners of the *Kirki* and with its underwriters. It was vital to get the *Kirki* away from the coast immediately in case she ran aground or broke up in the heavy seas.

Just after 10.30 a.m. the *Lady Kathleen* arrived at the site of the crippled tanker with the *Vigilant* not far behind. The wind and swell were still strong but in the clear daylight Farstad was able to get some idea of the task ahead. By this time 29 people had been rescued from the *Kirki*. The helicopters had to return to base to refuel and Captain Efstathopolous and the seven crew still on the tanker were waiting for their return. Anxious to get off the ship, Efstathopolous made the first of several requests for the *Lady Kathleen* to come alongside the *Kirki*, take the ship in tow and rescue the remaining crew. But Farstad had to consider the safety of his own crew and vessel. He told Efstathopolous that the conditions were too hazardous for the *Lady Kathleen* to be manoeuvred into such a position and encouraged the captain to wait for rescue when the helicopters returned. Failing that, he felt the best bet was for the crew members to jump into the water from where the crew of the tender could haul them aboard. But then the helicopters came into sight to complete the final stage of the rescue.

By the time the crew had reached safety, the contents of the *Kirki*'s two forward tanks had created an 29-kilometre oil slick around the ship. Captain Farstad on the *Lady Kathleen* was put in charge of towing the *Kirki* away from the coastline as soon as possible. But there was no one left on the tanker to pass or secure tow lines. The *Kirki* crew had left lines for the tow but one had been swept by the wind along the side of the ship and had become tangled, and the other was in such poor condition that it broke at the first attempt to secure it to the tug.

The only solution was to get some of the *Lady Kathleen*'s crew onto the *Kirki* to secure the lines. No jumping ladders had been put in place by the *Kirki's* crew, so Captain Farstad had to manoeuvre the *Lady Kathleen* close enough to the tanker to enable some of his crew to leap across onto the tanker's deck. It was a complex and dangerous manoeuvre executed with consummate skill. Three of the *Lady Kathleen*'s crew were soon aboard the stricken ship to perform the necessary task. By now the *Kirki* was just five nautical miles from the coastal shoal waters and the tow was underway just in time. The tanker was towed 62 nautical miles out to sea while plans were made regarding the nature of the salvage operation.

Between 10 and 20 000 tonnes of oil had already leaked

into the ocean and the oil was fast closing in on island nature reserves off Jurien Bay. The spillage was threatening a range of marine and bird life, particularly colonies of sea lions, as well as the multi-million dollar cray fishing industry—the livelihood of the coastal communities at Jurien and Cervantes.

Over the next couple of days the slick grew to 88 kilometres in length and 8 kilometres across its widest point. Captain Richard Purkiss of the Department of Marine and Harbours described the accident as a catastrophe of the worst proportions and the ensuing clean-up operation was massive. Within a couple of days nine million dollars' worth of clean-up equipment was flown to the area from the oil industry disaster centre in Geelong. Thousands of litres of dispersant were applied to the floating oil from the air. Helicopters positioned oil containment booms to protect the wildlife on the coastal islands which appeared to be under the greatest threat. A monitoring system was set up to keep watch over the wildlife, and nature also played its part as shore winds and choppy seas broke up some oil patches and drove them away from the land. Hundreds of volunteers, many of them from the coastal communities, gave their time to help with the clean-up. A week after the spill, water testing carried out by the Environmental Protection Authority showed that there was no increase in the presence of hydrocarbons in the water. Thanks to superb management, the massive clean-up had been a total success.

But what of the *Kirki*? While the crew of the *Lady Kathleen* had been getting her under tow, Captain David Hancox, the salvage master at United Salvage had made an aerial survey of the tanker. He needed assistance from the ship's senior officers but Captain Efstathopolous, who believed the *Kirki* was about to sink, refused permission. All that Hancox could get from the crew were some basic instructions and diagrams about the workings of the ship. When the salvage crew boarded the ship on 21 and 22 July they had to feel their own way, and under dangerous conditions. No ladders had been put out and the generators had been left running despite the risk of an explosion. The salvors' first task was to isolate the live electric cables which were dangling dangerously close to the leaking oil. And a decision had to be made regarding the fate of the *Kirki*.

Several options were dismissed. Dumping the oil at sea or scuttling the ship would create an environmental disaster of mammoth proportions. Towing her overseas would just be dumping the problem on someone else. The solution seemed to be to transfer the *Kirki*'s cargo to another vessel either at sea or off the north-west port of Dampier. Weather conditions made it far too dangerous to risk a transfer in the *Kirki*'s current location, so it was decided that the tanker should be towed to the sheltered waters of the North West Shelf where the transfer could be made under calmer conditions.

The task was huge—a tow of 1100 nautical miles involving a small fleet of vessels. The *Lady Elizabeth*, a tug from Fremantle, took over from the *Lady Kathleen* for the journey north, and while a slow and steady towing pace was maintained, the salvors worked to restore the *Kirki*'s safety systems and reduce the oil leakage. Plans were underway to transfer the 60 000 tonnes of oil still on board the *Kirki* to the tanker *Flying Clipper*, and salvage workers had their hands full preparing for the delicate operation. Pumps and cables were flown in by the RAAF from Brisbane and delivered to the *Kirki* by the tug *Pacific Chieftain*.

About two weeks after the tow began, the weather conditions began to deteriorate. The winds were blowing at 40 knots and there was a swell of four metres. The forward section of the *Kirki* started wearing down, three of the 16 tanks were full of water and three more were giving cause for concern. It was a struggle to keep the broken tanker afloat. All non-essential salvage personnel were moved off the *Kirki* to the *Pacific Chieftain* and the course was altered to seek shelter in the lee of the Montebello Islands. The *Kirki* was now 66 nautical miles off Dampier with 20 salvage workers on board, still risking their lives each day.

After reaching calmer waters, the operation to transfer the oil began. Fenders and cargo hoses were flown to the site but because there was no power on the *Kirki* the workers had to set the equipment in place manually. The excess water was discharged and more safety checks carried out to ensure there would be no accidental leaks. On 14 August the *Flying Clipper* was carefully manoeuvred so that her bow was to stern with the *Kirki*. Meanwhile the tug crew had to maintain tow speed to keep the damaged tanker alongside. As the oil was pumped from her tanks the *Kirki* rose in the water, and the extent of the damage could be seen for the first time. There were huge gaping holes in her hull where the forward section had broken away. By the evening of 17 August the transfer was completed and the oil was once again on its way to the Kwinana Refinery. The *Lady Elizabeth* towed the *Kirki* to Singapore where the hull was cleaned out and purchased by the Chinese for scrapping at Shanghai.

The greatest ever environmental threat to Australia's coastline had been averted and, just like the rescue, the salvage operation was a testament to the skill, dedication and courage of the many people and organisations involved. In the aftermath, there were criticisms regarding the *Kirki*'s condition when she set out on the voyage from the Gulf of Oman and the sorry state in which she had been left when her crew abandoned ship. But the rescue of 37 people from the *Kirki*, the subsequent clean-up and salvage are a proud chapter of Western Australia's sea rescue history.

Lone Yachtswoman

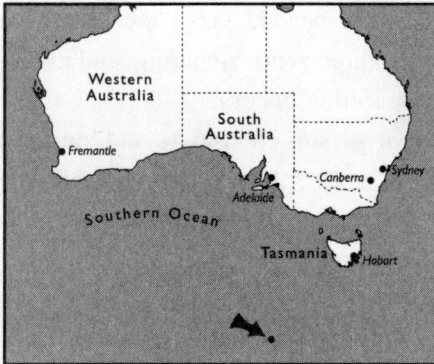

Rescue of Isabelle Autissier from the
Southern Ocean, 1 January 1995.

'This wave is dangerous!' Isabelle Autissier.

The impact of the massive wave was devastating. It had ripped a huge hole in the cabin roof, wiped out electronic equipment and destroyed the pump. Isabelle Autissier was determined she could still make it through to Sydney and began baling as fast as she could. The winds howled around the yacht and huge towers of water crashed across the deck. The icy cold wind and water numbed her body and the sight of her stricken boat broke her heart. She stopped baling and looked around her. It was impossible, the race was lost. She would never make the Australian coast now.

After an agonising decision in which her competitive spirit finally conceded to concern for her own safety and that of her boat, Isabelle Autissier activated the emergency

beacons on her crippled yacht. By triggering her own
rescue, Autissier had disqualified herself from the BOC
Challenge, a single-handed yacht race for which she had
spent more than three years preparing, and in which she had
already created sailing history.

What sort of person chooses to sail single-handed in a
race around the world? A race that will take them through
the most bleak and desolate oceans, in the most demanding
conditions? Why would you choose to risk your life, spend
months in isolation at sea, often facing a life and death battle
with the elements? It demands extraordinary courage, self-
reliance and strength of character, and that daredevil, risk-
taking streak that marks out the adventurer.

Isabelle Autissier is one of those people. An adventurer
and tough professional, she commands international respect
in the yachting world. An engineer and professor of marine
science from La Rochelle, France, Autissier was one of
three French entrants in the 1994/95 BOC Challenge and
the only woman in a field of 20 competitors from seven
countries. She has been sailing since she was seven years
old and her love of the ocean and yachts is matched by her
skill.

Originally a team sailor, she turned to solo racing as a
form of self-improvement in the late 1980s.

Inaugurated in 1982 by the American, David White, the
BOC is a formidable sailing challenge to both skipper and
yacht. The course is in four legs: Charleston, South Carolina
to Cape Town; Cape Town to Sydney; Sydney to Punta del
Este, Uruguay; then Punta del Este back to Charleston. The
race takes competitors through the world's oceans in the

toughest and most challenging sailing conditions. It demands rigorous practical planning and a commitment which spans several years of preparation. The 1994/95 Challenge was the fourth of its kind and the second attempt for Isabelle Autissier. In 1990/91 she became the first woman ever to finish the global classic. Despite the setback of a broken mast near the second leg of the race off the Tasmanian coast, she completed the course in 139 days, four hours and 48 minutes and finished seventh in her class. Her win captured the imagination and attention of people around the world.

Almost immediately after her 1990/91 success Isabelle Autissier began preparing for the 1994/95 race. For three years she worked with yacht designer Jean Beret and shipbuilder Marc Pinta on the *Ecureuil Poitu Charentes II*. The yacht, an 18-metre sloop valued at A$1.3 million, incorporated the most highly developed sailing technology and was her dream boat. Her next dream was to sail it in the BOC and win.

The 1994/95 Challenge started from Charleston on 17 September 1994. The 20 competitors and their yachts were divided into two classes and Isabelle Autissier and the *Ecureuil Poitou Charentes II* were in Class 1. She set sail on the 6865-mile first leg to Cape Town, where the estimated date of arrival for the first boats was 15 October.

Autissier headed out of Charleston sailing north and then east. A particularly good forecaster, she was able to cut through the Doldrums and avoid the calms which trap and frustrate many other competitors. She was off to a great start and her shore team rubbed their hands in glee as they monitored her position. Knowing she was in a commanding position, Autissier then took a risk spiced with intuition. As she approached the South Atlantic high pressure system 2000 nautical miles west of the Cape, she ignored the traditional course for Cape Town and set an early course southeast. The decision proved a winner. Autissier sailed the *Ecureuil Poitou Charentes II* into Cape Town on 24 October, a full five days ahead of her rivals. The voyage put her in the record books, for in addition to winning the first leg in Class 1, she had also sliced two days off the previous record. Autissier was amazed by her own success and could scarcely believe she had done it. Australian yachtsman, David Adams in his yacht *True Blue*, took the honours for Class 2. His respect for Autissier's sailing achievement was generously expressed and that respect was to increase in the second leg of the race.

The second leg of the BOC Challenge—the 6698 nautical miles to Sydney—got underway on 26 November. With a five-day lead, Isabelle Autissier could be permitted a feeling of assurance as she set out. But smug over-confidence was not her style. To bring her dream to reality, she needed all her nerve, experience and skill.

The Roaring Forties were named by the sailors who first ventured into the areas between 40 and 50 degrees latitude in the northern and southern hemispheres. The winds here blow across the oceans in a westerly direction and in the southern hemisphere, unimpeded by land mass, they are often strong to gale force throughout the year. On 2 December, Autissier was averaging more than 13 knots in the Roaring Forties, one of the loneliest and most dangerous ocean locations in the world. She had every reason to think she could head the field in the second leg when she heard a groaning wrench followed by a massive crash. A rigging screw had failed and the *Ecureuil*'s mast thundered down to the deck.

In the dark, early hours of the morning, Autissier cleared the debris off the deck to survey the damage. As the heavy rain lashed down and the 30-knot winds raged about her, she was overwhelmed by emotion. She knew she could no longer win the race but she struggled on, knowing that she was lucky to be safe. She radioed her situation back to France—a sad, almost resigned message—and affirmed her determination to make a safe landfall.

David Adams in the *True Blue* was 65 nautical miles from the *Ecureuil* and sailing in 40-knot winds. Race organisers rapidly identified him as the competitor closest to Autissier's position and at 1200 GMT, he was asked to change course and head for the damaged yacht located south of Marion Island. Night was falling when Adams reached Autissier. She was standing on the deck—a tiny solitary figure—as the damaged yacht pitched wildly in the seas. Adams made one pass of the long-keeled yacht and lowered his sails so that they could speak across the swell, their words sweeping upwards on the howling winds. Autissier was grateful to Adams for diverting from his course in order to come to her aid, but she was determined to continue alone. One of the rules of the BOC race is that contestants cannot rely on outside assistance if they get into trouble. There was little that Adams could have done to help Autissier in that situation.

Autissier told Adams that she would continue on without help. She intended to build a jury rig—a makeshift rigging—which would take her as far as the Kerguelen Islands. The dismasted, long-keeled *Ecureuil* was rolling furiously in the wild conditions as Adams raised his sails and once again set a course for Sydney. The incident had moved him deeply and he sailed away feeling shattered by the enormity of the task Autissier was about to undertake.

As Adams disappeared out of sight, Autissier went back to work. With an enormous effort she built the jury rig and set course for the Kerguelens. To sail her yacht under jury rig for the next two weeks, Autissier had to draw upon all her knowledge and intuition. It was a torturous journey and during the latter part of the run she had to battle 40-knot winds and heavy snow. Averaging between 100 and 160 nautical miles a day, Autissier finally reached the southern end of the islands. Once there, things took a turn for the better. A team of French scientists on the vessel *Curieuse* was conducting technological studies in the Antarctic region and was on hand to help. While Isabelle Autissier battled her way out of the Roaring Forties, her shore team found her a new 43-metre mast on the Reunion Islands. A supply ship on its way to the Kerguelens picked up the new mast, and more ropes, sails and other rigging had been despatched by air from France.

Autissier was deeply disappointed that she would not be able to make it to Sydney by Christmas. Nevertheless, she threw herself into the task of getting the mast fitted to her boat. She had spent the early part of the race counting the days which separated her from the other contestants, and

despite having lost her advantage, her spirit and commitment were as strong as ever. In a race like the BOC, Autissier knew that anything was possible. It was still a long way
to the finish in Charleston but perhaps her luck would
change again.

Autissier was deeply moved by the way people rallied
to help her. Local islanders and the French scientists threw
their efforts and support behind her and her spirits and
energy surged as she began repairing the yacht. The replace-
ment mast had been made for a cruising ship and she
decided to convert the *Ecureuil* from a single-masted sloop
to a double-masted yawl. When the work was completed
she had a mainmast which was 13 metres long, and had
fashioned a mizzen mast from her spinnaker pole. It was
going to be difficult to use because the *Ecureuil*'s sails were
not built for such a rig, but she was thrilled with the result
nonetheless. Now she could get going again. At 7.30 GMT
on 16 December, just three days after limping into the
island's southern bay, Autissier was at sea again. She had
worked non-stop alongside her supporters and now she was
determined to make the fastest speed possible to Australia.

Knowing that the sail on the *Ecureuil*'s new mast was not
large enough to give her the speed she wanted in light winds,
Autissier made a bid for stronger conditions by heading south.
It was here that the weather took a turn for the worse. During
the night of Tuesday, 27 December, the winds were up to 50
and 60 knots and enormous waves were breaking across the
Ecureuil's deck. With no sails up, Autissier was travelling at
8 knots. The next day there was no let-up in the weather but
the yacht was still travelling well. Autissier was at the back

of the boat in a narrow protected passage when she heard the sound of an oncoming wave, like nothing she had ever heard before. 'I heard the wave coming like a big roar. I thought this wave is dangerous, but of course I could do nothing,' she said. The wave crashed into the boat, tearing a hole in the roof of the cabin, and sending Autissier hurtling on her side, then onto the ceiling.

The yacht went into a roll and water poured in through the broken roof. As the boat swung up out of the roll, Autissier struggled to her feet in the cabin. She had to work fast to fix a sail across the five-metre hole in the cabin roof to prevent more water from coming in. Once again, she counted herself lucky to be alive. Had she been on deck she would have been swept away with no hope of survival. Even if she had been in her berth or sitting at the chart table she could have been swept out as the roof was ripped away. Having fixed the roof the next job was to assess the extent of the damage caused by the freak wave. She had no radio contact and the *Ecureuil*'s steering system along with some other electronic equipment was broken. The rear bulkhead was destroyed, the aft compartment of the yacht was leaking and the pump was inoperable. There was no denying that Autissier's situation was disastrous.

The BOC yacht race has a tradition of disasters and heroism and demands high standards of its competitors. People who race yachts solo are fiercely self-reliant and in eight years of sailing, Isabelle Autissier had never needed rescuing. It was understandable, therefore, that she spent a considerable amount of time agonising over whether she should ask for help. Not only would a distress call be at odds with the spirit of the race, it would also mean disqualification. More significantly, she would be asking others to put their lives at risk in an attempt to rescue her. Autissier had spent three years building the boat and planning for the race. Her attachment to the *Ecureuil* was very strong and she wanted to do something—anything—to stay on board and sail her safely to Australia. But the time had come to acknowledge that her dream was over. At 06.45 GMT on Wednesday, 28 December, two hours after the freak wave, Autissier switched on her Electronic Position Indicating Radio Beacon (EPIRB).

Autissier was around 850 nautical miles south-west of Hobart, adrift in the Southern Ocean. Having set off the beacons, she cleared away the broken masts, sails and rigging from the deck. Both the masts were down and she secured a portion of the main spar on the deck. She checked the sail covering the gaping hole in the cabin roof and then baled water from the yacht with a bucket. Cold and wet, despite her survival suit, Autissier managed to find a dry spot in the sail storage compartment. Carefully, she stowed all the food and clothing she could find and crawled into the tiny space. As the *Ecureuil* was battered by ten-metre seas and winds raging between 50 and 60 knots, Autissier kept a lonely vigil on her yacht. All she could do now was wait for help to arrive. It would be 18 hours before she saw the first signs of a rescue on its way.

The Rescue Coordination Centre in Canberra had picked up the *Ecureuil*'s distress signal and immediately set about activating plans for a rescue. As soon as it was light the RAAF despatched a Hercules C-130 aircraft from Richmond

Air Base in Sydney to the estimated location in the Southern Ocean. The search was a formidable task, with strong winds and driving rain limiting visibility. The Hercules had the latest electronic search equipment on board but in the end it was the naked eyes of the crew that spotted the damaged yacht. At 00.45 GMT on the morning of Thursday, 29 December, they caught sight of the *Ecureuil* floating perilously in the wild seas.

Isabelle Autissier's spirits had swung between hope and despair that lonely night in the Southern Ocean. As she heard the Hercules flying overhead, she scrambled out onto the deck waving to the crew with a feeling of immense relief. Flying in 60-knot winds, the Hercules successfully dropped a life raft and a canister filled with survival items almost into her hands. Autissier lashed the life raft to the side of the *Ecureuil* and after a second successful drop she was able to establish radio communication. She told the crew she was sad and cold but had enough food for one day and about four litres of water. Not wanting to let the yacht out of its sight, the RAAF despatched Orion aircraft from Edinburgh Air Base in South Australia to circle the yacht. Autissier's spirits were lifted by the consistent presence of the Orions overhead. They were a reassuring reminder that rescue was simply a matter of time. The flying time from Edinburgh Air Base to the yacht's location was around three hours and the Orion crews flew six-hour watches before returning to base. It was dangerous and demanding flying and required intense concentration in hazardous conditions over extended periods. But to Autissier, the sight of the Orions was her precious link to hope.

Although the weather conditions eased slightly, Autissier's vigil on the crippled *Ecureuil* was a cold and lonely one. Wind and water temperatures were just a few degrees above freezing and there was only a tiny dry space on the water-logged yacht. Autissier was cramped and freezing and her heart was heavy with the loss of her hopes and dreams. The time seemed interminable and there was little she could do to distract herself. Vigilance was combined with sadness, boredom and the terrible frustration of not being able to help herself. She eked out her food and water, knowing that anything could happen to delay the expected rescue, and she kept watch on her boat and the weather.

Meanwhile, under direction from the Rescue Coordination Centre, a guided missile frigate of the Australian Navy, the HMAS *Darwin*, set out to rendezvous with the stricken yacht. At 11.30 GMT on Friday, 30 December the frigate left her berth at Garden Island off Fremantle under the command of Davyd Thomas. On board the frigate was a Seahawk class helicopter, as well as a doctor and a French interpreter. The plan was to get within about 185 kilometres of the *Ecureuil*, then launch the Seahawk which would fly to the yacht and winch Autissier to safety. The operation was dependent on the weather: if the seas were too rough the Seahawk would not be able to take off or land. A low pressure system with an associated front was moving towards the yacht from 740 kilometres to the east, so HMAS *Darwin* was racing to the scene at maximum speed in an attempt to beat the deteriorating weather. The rendezvous was planned for 3.30 a.m. local time and Commander Thomas was confident they would reach the *Ecureuil* before the front was due to pass through on Sunday. Sure enough, at first light, the Seahawk took off from the HMAS *Darwin* in 20-knot winds and flew towards the *Ecureuil*.

As the sun rose on the Southern Ocean and a new year dawned, Isabelle Autissier saw her rescuers. Standing on the deck of her tossing yacht in her red survival suit, she watched as the huge frigate steadily approached. The helicopter which would lift her from the yacht was flying towards her and overhead an Orion continued to circle. For the woman who had spent four lonely days in the desolate heart of the Southern Ocean, the sight of so many people coming to her aid was overwhelming. The Seahawk drew closer until it was hovering as low as possible above the yacht. A crew member was lowered to the deck of the *Ecureuil* and Autissier raised her arms to struggle into the harness. Clutching only a small bag of personal belongings, she was winched to safety in the body of the Seahawk. As the helicopter turned and banked, Autissier watched the yacht which had held all her dreams and hopes become just a small white speck, bobbing and rolling in the huge seas.

It was only a short flight back to the deck of the HMAS *Darwin*. But despite her gruelling four-day ordeal, Autissier was in good shape and she was able to enjoy a hot shower and tuck into a breakfast of bacon and eggs. Later she met with the crew of the frigate and thanked them for their valiant efforts. The following day, as the HMAS *Darwin* neared Adelaide, Autissier again boarded the Seakhawk helicopter and flew to the RAAF Edinburgh base. Even in the immediate aftermath of her brush with disaster, Autissier's spirit was still strong and only moments after setting foot on dry land she vowed to continue ocean sailing. Later at a media conference she praised her rescuers for a perfect job.

'All the time you guys were just above me, just circling above me and that was a great help ... it got very difficult down there. I am here because of you and I will never forget that,' she told her rescuers. 'I was really confident and I know I was true to be confident in you.'

But Autissier was still concerned for her yacht. As she pointed out, it was the first time she had come ashore without her boat. A part of her remained with the *Ecureuil* and she was determined to retrieve the yacht. But it was not to be. While Isabelle Autissier enjoyed the relief of a warm and dry night's sleep aboard HMAS *Darwin*, the Hobart-based deep sea trawler *Petunia* set out to locate her yacht and salvage it. But attempts to find the yacht proved fruitless and a few days later the search was abandoned. The *Ecureuil* is believed to have sunk or drifted south, beyond the range of reasonable salvage.

The defence forces' rescue of Isabelle Autissier received international attention and praise. In Australia, the cost of the rescue sparked a heated debate. Originally estimated at about one million dollars, it was later stated to be closer to five million. The Australian Government accepted financial responsibility for the rescue as a fulfilment of its international obligations, alongside the well deserved praise for its defence forces.

As for the lone yachstwoman, Isabelle Autissier was at sea again a year later as a contestant in the 1996/97 Vendee Globe race—a race which created some spectacular Southern Ocean rescues of its own.

The 1996/97 Vendee Globe
Rescues in the Southern Ocean

The Vendee Globe solo round-the-world yacht race is the ultimate challenge for lone sailors. It is more demanding and dangerous than any other race and is the most prestigious test of single-handed sailing in the world. The race was established by Philippe Jeantot, one of the world's most respected single-handed ocean racers, and involves an unassisted non-stop race on 15- to 18-metre, single-hulled vessels. Jeantot wanted to establish a non-stop contest in which the rhythm would not be broken by port stops, as in the BOC race. Entry requirements for the Vendee Globe race are rigorous and competitors must first complete a single-handed voyage of 10 000 nautical miles. In the 1996/97 race only five competitors, one of whom was Isabelle Autissier, had experience of sailing single-handed in the Southern Ocean.

The race attracts risk takers and adventurers who revel in pitting their knowledge and skills against the most extreme forces of nature. Starting from the Atlantic coast of France at Sables d'Olonne in the Vendee Region, the race takes it competitors through the Atlantic, around the Cape of Good Hope, deep into the Southern Ocean between the south coast of Australia and the north of Antarctica, back up past Cape Horn, and northwards through the Atlantic back to Sables d'Olonne. The conditions vary from the calm waters in the equatorial regions, to the wild and desolate reaches of the Roaring Forties and the Furious Fifties, a bleak place with steel grey skies and howling gales. The waves here can reach the height of a four-storey building and water temperatures border on freezing all year round. Sometimes called the Kerguelen Triangle, this area is the site of a convergence of currents which creates potentially lethal cross seas, and is known to many sailors as the 'sea of certain death'.

In December 1996 and January 1997, international attention was focused on the rescue of three Vendee Globe competitors in the Southern Ocean. The stories of Raphael Dinelli, Theirry Dubois and Tony Bullimore filled the news headlines and the world watched transfixed as the Australian defence forces and solo yachtsman Pete Goss carried out the dramatic rescue operations. The 1996/97 Vendee Globe Southern Ocean rescues will take their place in the history books, and have brought well deserved international prestige and praise to the Australian defence forces. The rescues are stories of outstanding skill and seamanship, brilliant flying, superb management and coordination, and are inspiring examples of the courage and endurance of the human spirit. Sadly the 1996/97 Vendee Globe was also marked by tragedy. Canadian skipper Gerry Roufs in his yacht *Group LGII* lost contact with race headquarters on 7 January when he was about 2500 nautical miles west of New Zealand. Roufs is believed to have been lost at sea.

The winner of the 1996/97 Vendee Globe round-the-world race was Frenchman Christophe Augin in the sloop *Geodis*. Augin completed the race in a record 106 days, 1500 nautical miles ahead of the next competitor. But Augin's triumph was upstaged somewhat by the dramatic rescues of Dinelli, Dubois and Bullimore, and marred by the loss of Gerry Roufs.

Knee-deep on a Sinking Yacht

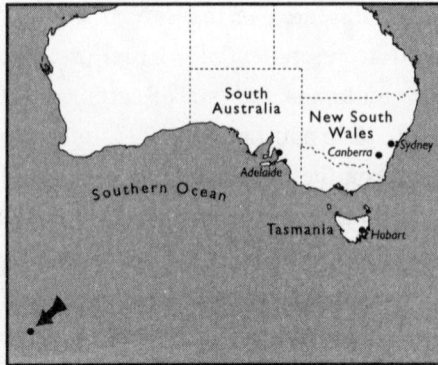

The rescue of Raphael Dinelli from the
Southern Ocean, 28 December 1996.

*'I have just had the best Christmas present
ever. Raphael is on board.'* Fellow Vendee
Globe competitor Pete Goss.

Raphael Dinelli struggled to keep his balance on the
deck of his capsized yacht. Huge waves crashed over
him as he moved cautiously towards his only hope of survival, the life raft. But to his horror, the raft broke free of
its rope right before his eyes and was swept out of his reach.
Dinelli was entirely alone more than 1250 nautical miles
from the south-west coast of Australia. He was in the depths
of the Southern Ocean, the loneliest place on earth. As the
seas pounded and the winds blew at 40 knots, Dinelli was
standing knee-high in icy water on the deck of his sinking
yacht and it was taking all his strength just to stay there. It
could be hours, even days before anyone found him.

Perhaps he was too far away to be rescued, maybe no one was even looking for him. He could only wait and hope.

Hours earlier, while most people were opening their Christmas presents, Raphael Dinelli and Pete Goss were battling raging seas and winds gusting furiously at 70 knots. They were in the heart of the Furious Fifties, an area more desolate and inhospitable than the Roaring Forties where the size of the waves can smash a yacht to pieces and where great chunks of ice loom out of the darkness. More than 150 nautical miles separated the two men as they pitted themselves against the elements in a region known to sailors as the 'sea of certain death'.

Goss and Dinelli were racing in the most gruelling leg of the Vendee Globe round-the-world yacht race. Goss was an official competitor but Dinelli had been denied official status as he had failed to complete a qualifier in the required time. Refusing to take no for an answer, Dinelli decided to sail the race route along with the rest of the fleet. At 28 years of age, the Frenchman from Aquitaine was the youngest skipper in the race and had been sailing for 12 years. Dinelli's 18-metre chartered yacht the *Algimouss* had already sailed twice around the world. Formerly named the *Credit Agricole 4* it was designed and raced by the man who started the Vendee Globe and who is now its director, Phillipe Jeantot. For Englishman Pete Goss, a former naval instructor and highly experienced yachtsman, this was his first solo round-the-world race. At 15 metres, his yacht *Aqua Quorum* was smaller than most other contestants' boats, and he was confident that it would be the fastest and most reliable of the Vendee Globe fleet.

Dinelli and Goss hardly knew each other when the race began but as the yachts rounded the tip of the Cape of Good Hope the two became acquainted over the radio. Goss's satellite fax broke down, cutting him off from communications with race headquarters. Dinelli kept in touch with him, relaying messages for several days until Goss's fax was fixed.

The weather on Christmas Day started off reasonably well with 20-knot winds from the north. But as the day wore on, conditions began to change. The winds increased to 60 knots and the seas grew bigger with strong cross swells. The *Algimouss* had been knocked down several times in the furious conditions and Dinelli had been struggling all night to keep control. He decided to run before the wind and set two sea anchors designed for a much larger vessel. But even with no sails the ferocious winds were driving the *Algimouss* at tremendous speed, sending her surfing down the mountainous waves.

By the evening Dinelli was in a state of near exhaustion. He had just sat down at his computer table when the *Algimouss* was suddenly swept up by a huge wave and sent surfing faster than ever before. In seconds the gauge reached 26 knots. As the yacht shot down to the base of the wave, she was hurled up again. There was an ear splitting crash and Dinelli was thrown upside down. He landed on the ceiling which was where the floor should have been, and the seat he had been sitting on was ripped from its fixings. At first he was stunned and couldn't understand what had happened. As he looked around he realised that the yacht had completely capsized. The mast had broken off at its base and been thrust straight through into the sail locker. Because the mast was still vertical the boat could not right herself and the huge hole in the deck grew larger each time the waves battered the boat and caused the mast to crash from side to side.

Dinelli pulled himself together and surveyed the damage. The *Algimouss* was leaking badly, water was pouring in and flooding each compartment. A diesel tank had blown open and the fuel was gushing out. The fumes were overwhelming and Dinelli soon started to vomit. He quickly plugged the diesel tank and closed all the bulkhead hatches. Most of the contents of the cabin were floating in the water around his feet. Dinelli knew his situation was desperate. He needed to get out of the cabin but there was no way he could do that until the boat righted herself. He rummaged around to find an ARGOS beacon and set it off, but he feared it was unlikely to work effectively through the hull of the boat.

Thoughts of dying alone in that wild and hostile place crept into Dinelli's mind but he drove them out and began to prepare himself for when the boat was upright and he could go outside. He put on his survival suit and found some more distress beacons and some food. Until the boat righted herself, Dinelli would have to stay in the tiny cabin, which was steadily filling with water, and with each passing minute the air space was running out. Dinelli sat in the cramped, flooding space and wondered if he would get out before it was completely flooded with water. It took three whole hours before the force of the waves finally ripped the mast right out of the upturned yacht and she rolled upright again on the swell.

Dinelli scrambled out onto the deck in relief and immediately set off his EPIRB. Then he secured the life raft and put his survival kit into it. By now the stern was awash with waves and water was cascading past him. The prospect of staying on deck was terrifying, but the combination of the swell and the water filling the hull had broken all the windows and there was no way he could go back inside the boat. Dinelli thought he might be able to keep the boat afloat a bit longer by blocking the ballast tank vents. It might make only a slight difference, but in those circumstances anything was worth a try. It was at this point, when Dinelli turned to the leeward, that he saw the raft had broken away from the yacht and was now out of reach. He was alone on a sinking yacht, hundreds of miles from anywhere in the most appalling conditions imaginable. The *Algimouss* was partially submerged and as Dinelli stood on the deck, he was knee-deep in icy cold water. The bow was the only part of the yacht still above the water. Dinelli fastened his harness and attached himself to the gooseneck. With 70-knot winds screaming around him and 24-metre waves continually breaking over him, Raphael Dinelli began the longest wait of his life.

One hundred and sixty nautical miles to the south, Pete Goss was running with just a storm jib before a fearsome south-westerly. Like Dinelli, Goss had been struggling for hours to control his yacht and he had been knocked down three times. Once again, he was flung to the floor as the *Aqua Quorum* was flattened onto her side and all the lights cut out. As he hung on in the darkness and hoped for the best, a tremendous crashing wave smashed the yacht over again and sent a chill of fear through his bones. The *Aqua Quorum* seemed to sigh under the pressure of the knock down. Goss was sure the yacht would roll over but then he felt the sway upwards as she righted herself once again.

Before Goss had time to take stock of his situation the Satcom bleeped a mayday referred by the Rescue Coordination Centre in Canberra. Someone was obviously in worse trouble than him. A satellite telex arrived from Paris and informed him that his colleague, Raphael Dinelli had put out the SOS. Another competitor, Patrick de Radigues, was closer to the location but his power generator had been smashed by the storm and the race organisers could not contact him. Goss was being asked to go and help the French skipper.

Pete Goss was devastated. He had spent many dangerous hours fighting his way through this horrific storm and now he was being asked to turn around and head back into it. Dinelli's position was north-north-west of Goss so he would be travelling broadside to the wind and swell. Goss was already at the limits of his energy and he sat for a few minutes contemplating the task ahead. He wondered if it would even be possible to make any progress through the storm, but in the end he knew he had to go back. It was a matter of responsibility and his training as a Royal Marine had prepared him to perform with efficiency and professionalism.

As Goss braced himself for the torturous journey back through the storm, race organisers in Paris were alerting the Australian Maritime Safety Authority (AMSA) to the emergency. (ARGOS beacons do not comply with international standards and signal only to France.) It was 1.30 a.m. on Boxing Day when Flying Officer Andy Bennett, the Duty Operations Officer with the 92 Wing of the RAAF, received the telephone call which would trigger the air search for Dinelli. A number 10 Squadron crew, captained by Flight Lieutenant Ian Whyte, would conduct the search. A large number of personnel were on Christmas leave and had to be recalled, but the crew was rapidly assembled and 12 squadron members took off in an Orion P 3 Rescue 251 from Edinburgh Air Base in South Australia. The aircraft stopped to refuel in Perth before heading out over the ocean to begin the search.

Just after 1.00 a.m. Pete Goss made the first manoeuvre to take him back towards Dinelli. He gybed and it went without a hitch. The *Aqua Quorum* was travelling at a speed of eight knots and Goss sent a fax to Paris confirming that he was on his way to assist his stricken colleague. The journey was a nightmare. Goss pressed on through many knock downs, one of which took the mast down to 90 degrees. After an agonising wait, she slowly righted herself but she had lost the spinnaker pole and more water was sweeping into the cabin. Objects were being hurled around the cabin and were floating in the water on the floor. A container of cooking oil had burst open and was spreading rapidly, making the cabin slippery and even more dangerous. Huge waves were sweeping down the deck and raking open the hatches. Goss, cold, hungry and sleep-deprived, but knew there would be hours more of these conditions ahead of him.

In the chaos of the cabin, Goss managed to find some

food then strapped himself into a bunk to rest. He woke a short while later to further chaos. An aerosol can of oil had broken loose and become trapped between the terminals of the generator. This had caused the generator to short circuit and huge sparks were crackling from it. The oily contents of the can was floating on the surface of water in the cabin. Goss sent another fax to Paris asking for the latest weather forecast, then he strapped himself back into his bunk and tried to sleep again. But his thoughts turned to Dinelli. Was he still with the boat or had he taken to the raft by now? He had no idea what his friend's situation might be, only that there was another 80 nautical miles still between them. Another 80 nautical miles of unbelievable storm which was pushing Goss to the limits.

Raphael Dinelli was still standing on the deck of the *Algimouss*. The waves were continually knocking him head-long into the freezing cold water. Time after time Dinelli struggled back to his feet which, along with his legs, were numb from the cold. Hour after hour passed until the first light of dawn appeared, the harsh brightness illuminating the empty horizons.

As the waves continued to pummel the yacht, the final watertight compartment yielded. Now the *Algimouss* was level under the water and slowly sinking lower. Dinelli knew the boat was taking him down too, but there was no-where else for him to go. He knew that no other competitor was near enough to reach him and, given the conditions, a helicopter rescue was impossible. The thought of dying haunted him. He thought about his life and the people he loved, his baby and his partner Virginie Glory.

As the seemingly endless day wore on, Dinelli remained
fixed to the deck. He was frozen and encrusted with salt.
His lips were swollen and burning and he was half blinded
by the wind and salt. In the afternoon, the winds lessened
slightly to about 40 knots but the huge waves were still
breaking on and around him. The air temperature was zero
but the windchill factor made it much lower. Dinelli's eyes
were swollen now and almost closed. He did not know how
he was still alive. So many times he had thought that he
was at the end of his endurance, that he could not go on
any longer. But somehow the minutes and the hours ticked
away and he was still there, still holding on, still waiting to
die. The light was fading. He stood like a downhill skier
with his feet planted firmly and knees slightly bent, as it
was the only way to maintain a sense of stability. He knew
that at any minute the *Algimouss* could sink. He would not
be able to survive much longer, with or without the yacht.

And then there it was—a miracle! Overhead, Dinelli
heard the sound of an aircraft and it was as if the blood
started to flow through his body again. He had been standing on his yacht for 22 hours. The RAAF Orion passed
across him several times, circling him. It had taken them
almost five and a half hours to find him, a tiny orange speck
on the surface of the ocean with the dark shape of the *Algimouss* beneath him. As Dinelli waved and watched, the
crew calculated the crucial drop of the survival kit. It needed
to be fairly accurate so that he would be able to reach the
kit. The aircraft descended to 90 metres above sea level and,
flying at 160 knots, dropped two containers linked by a rope
impressively close to the lone yachtsman.

Dinelli was able to grab the line and the life raft, which had inflated on impact with the water. Staggering and sliding across the deck, he managed to haul himself into the raft and had a look to see what was there. He knew he had to eat in order to keep going—the wait for a ship to reach him could take a long time. But there was no food in the raft. Painfully, he climbed back onto the *Algimouss* and opened the locker where he had stored some supplies. He reached in with his legs and managed to fish out a container of food. With his frozen and aching feet he felt around for some drinking water. He couldn't feel any and just as he was about to pull his legs out, a bottle of champagne floated up from the locker. He caught it and, clutching his provisions tightly, staggered back into the raft.

Dinelli was saved with just seconds to spare. As he got into the raft, the *Algimouss* quietly disappeared beneath the water. It was almost as though she had been waiting for him to step onto the raft before finally giving up the ghost. Dinelli was overwhelmed with sadness at the loss of the yacht, and with relief at his own extraordinary last minute escape. But there was little time for him to reflect. The Orion dropped another two packages from overhead and despite the chilling pain in his arms, Dinelli paddled with his hands to reach one. It contained the message that Goss was on his way to pick him up but was still ten hours away.

Dinelli baled some water out of the raft and set up his ARGOS beacon. His throat was aching for a drink so he decided to open the champagne. His hands were near frozen and it was a long and painful task. At last the cork was out of the bottle but it was agony to drink. The sharp gaseous liquid seared his burnt and swollen lips. The champagne was the only fluid he had to drink so he had to ration its intake. Using a knife, he slowly and painfully cut down the cork to force it back into the bottle. It was almost dark now and still many hours before he could expect Goss. Outside, two albatrosses started to dive at the raft. Dinelli was terrified that they would puncture it with their beaks or claws, and he splashed and screamed at them to stop it. For an hour the birds took turns attacking the raft and the beacon before they eventually flew off.

Water had found its way inside his survival suit and Dinelli was shivering with cold. His body was throbbing with pain and every movement he made was agony. He opened some food and weakly managed to eat something. He was trying to keep the contents of the survival kit together as he was thrown about by the waves. The life raft was like a tiny bubble in the huge seas. Dinelli lay back in the raft to stretch out his stiff, sore body. Outside it was pitch dark and the swell was getting stronger. Dinelli's teeth were chattering uncontrollably. Then his legs and arms, his head and finally his whole body began to shake as the hypothermia, exhaustion and terror took hold of him.

Pete Goss had survived the storm with only a broken mainsail. After repairing it he went below deck to grab a can of cold baked beans, and this was when he heard the engines of the Orion aircraft. The Orion crew relayed to Goss that Dinelli was alive and in his survival suit in a life raft. After receiving the exact location for Dinelli, Goss sat down to work out how he was going to reach him. The weather forecast was not good and the head winds, big seas and poor visibility were expected to continue. From his charts Goss could see that he was just 20 nautical miles directly downwind of Dinelli's position. He travelled on through the night, short tacking to cope with the weather.

In the next five hours Goss travelled 15 nautical miles only to find on the next position check that Dinelli's location had changed dramatically in the night and he had actually overshot the new position. Goss turned again and headed back, following the drift line. When he reached the precise location there was no sign of Dinelli. Goss sailed slowly under a storm jib. The wind had grown even more fierce and the visibility was terrible, but by all indications Dinelli must be very close. Goss yelled out, fired rocket flares and blasted the foghorn. Perhaps Dinelli had fallen asleep. If Goss could wake him Dinelli could set off a flare to guide the yacht closer to his raft.

Zigzagging on down the drift line, Goss searched in vain. He went below deck to check the position and it had changed again. Stress and exhaustion were making it hard for Goss to take in what was happening. Desperately, he plotted the location and found himself a horrifying 50 nautical miles off target. He tried again and this time he got it right—he was only six nautical miles away. As daylight broke Goss went up on deck and saw the RAAF Rescue 252 Orion aircraft. Over the radio the Orion crew told Goss that they had spotted Dinelli waving to them from the raft and that they would guide Goss to him. Goss was overwhelmed with relief and the excitement of being close to his target. The last two miles became one mile and soon he could see the raft. Goss began to position himself so that he would approach the life raft on the port side.

Thirty-six hours after he had broadcast his mayday, Dinelli saw the *Aqua Quorum* racing towards him. At first it appeared as an indistinguishable speck, then it grew larger, taking shape as it pressed on through the enormous waves. The distance between Dinelli and Goss was rapidly closing until Dinelli was finally able to grasp the line and feel Goss heave him up the side of the *Aqua Quorum*. Dinelli fell face down on the deck, too cold and stiff to move. Goss turned him over and the two men hugged each other with relief. In the raft, Dinelli had been curled up in a foetal position. Now his body had locked rigid with cold and exhaustion and he could not straighten himself. Goss had to drag Dinelli to the cockpit by his ankles to get him out of the wind and water breaking over the deck. He quickly put up the storm jib to steady the roll on the yacht, then returned to his casualty.

Dinelli's feet and hands were stiff and colourless. His eyes were swollen and waxy, and his body was rigid as though he had rigor mortis. Goss had to manoeuvre him like a piece of furniture to the cabin below, where he propped him up with pillows, wrapped him in a sleeping bag with a hot water bottle, and gave him hot drinks. Both men were rendered almost speechless by the enormity of their experience. Dinelli was awed by the reality of his survival and Goss was heady with the joy of his friend's safety. Over the radio Goss told the rescue coordinators, 'I have just had the best Christmas present ever. Raphael is on board.'

But the rescue was not over. The *Aqua Quorum* was still around 1200 nautical miles from the Australian coast, closer in fact to Antarctica. It would take more than a week to reach Hobart and Goss and Dinelli were both already completely exhausted. Nevertheless Goss soldiered on and set a course for Hobart. He received some physiotherapy instruction from medical professionals over the radio and cared for his colleague until, after four days, Dinelli was finally able to straighten his body and move again.

The ten-day run to Hobart allowed time for Dinelli's spirit to ease and he could begin to talk to Goss about those endless hours standing on his yacht and his time in the life raft. In fact, once he started talking, he couldn't stop. He was trying to make sense of it and it aided his recovery to talk about it. By the time Goss and Dinelli sailed into Hobart the two men had forged a strong friendship. As Goss sailed out of Hobart a few days later to begin the next leg of the race, Dinelli told Goss, 'My heart is with your heart.'

Pete Goss finished fifth in the Vendee Globe race and was awarded the British Royal Ocean Racing Club's trophy for outstanding seamanship, as well as the Legion d'Honneur, France's most prestigious award. Despite his close encounter with death, Raphael Dinelli vowed to sail again. 'I love sailing now and I need to (be) sailing because it's my life,' he said. While he was standing on his sinking yacht he vowed that if he survived his ordeal he would ask his girlfriend, Virginie Glory, to marry him—his proposal was accepted.

While Goss risked his life to save Dinelli, he could not have done it without the outstanding search effort of the

RAAF Orion crew and the Rescue Coordination Centre. And a few days after they had spotted Dinelli, they were once again searching the Southern Ocean for two more lone yachtsmen, which became the most dramatic rescue operation in yachting history.

Two Miracle Rescues

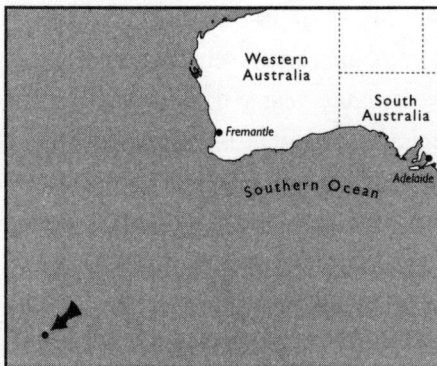

Rescue of Thierry Dubois and Tony
Bullimore from the Southern Ocean,
9 January 1997.

*'Thank you Australia for giving me back my
life!'* Tony Bullimore.

Pictures of Raphael Dinelli standing on his sinking yacht, alone in the vast and threatening expanse of the Southern Ocean, had been flashed around the world. They were pictures to stop even the most cynical in their tracks. Dinelli had been standing for 22 hours, waiting and hoping to be rescued. This surely was the epitome of courage and determination, a marathon of human endurance. And then the world watched as Pete Goss risked everything to rescue Dinelli and took him to safety on his own yacht. Adventurers and heroes—the two men grabbed the hearts and minds of far more than just the yachting enthusiasts. But there was more to come. While Goss and Dinelli were making their way to Hobart on the *Aqua Quorum*, another two lone yachtsmen were heading for disaster in the Southern Ocean.

Tony Bullimore, a 58-year-old gritty and pugnacious Englishman, has an earthy sense of humour and an open manner. Twenty-nine-year-old Thierry Dubois, on the other hand, is a quiet and thoughtful Frenchman who only speaks when he has something to say. Within a few days these two very different men became the heroes of a drama which had people around the world glued to their television screens. Their fate galvanised the international community in an hour-by-hour, day-by-day, world-wide rescue watch.

Bullimore and Dubois both had an overwhelming passion to sail in and win the Vendee Globe solo round-the-world yacht race. It was the most exacting test of their seamanship and endurance and represented the ultimate challenge. Bullimore is a popular and very experienced British yachtsman, one of a rare breed of adventurers who constantly confronts fate. From the deserts of Africa to the desolate horizons of the ocean, he is no stranger to life-threatening situations. In 1992, Bullimore built his 20-metre ketch, the *Global Exide Challenger* in accordance with the strict requirements of the Vendee Globe race. The boat was to be self-righting and unsinkable—and he almost got it right. Thierry Dubois hails from Brittany, France, and is an intense and determined man. He is a highly experienced navigator and lone sailor, but the 1996/97 Vendee Globe in *Pour Amnesty International* was to be his first round-the-world race.

The race competitors left the starting point at Les Sables d'Olonne on 3 November, 1996. Two days later, Tony

Bullimore discovered a fuel leak and had to turn back. He was on his way again by 7 November. Dubois also experienced a hitch soon after the start. Just as he was approaching the Spanish coast, he hit a large floating object and had to turn back. He left again on 9 November, two days behind Bullimore. Frustrating though the delays must have been, they were nothing compared to the trouble they were to experience a couple of months later.

On Sunday, 5 January, Dubois and Bullimore were battling it out in the Roaring Forties. As the day wore on the weather conditions became extreme. The two skippers were facing 65-knot winds and waves that were like massive walls of water. Thierry Dubois had been thinking about the rescue of Dinelli the week before and was cautious about gathering too much speed—at times the anemometer showed the wind speed rising to 70 knots. Dubois decided to go below and leave the yacht on pilot. *Pour Amnesty International* was taking a massive beating in the stormy sea. Several times she was knocked down on her side and sometimes she was knocked even further so that her mast disappeared under the water. Each time the knock downs sent Dubois flying around the cabin.

Then it happened. The yacht took off at massive speed on a wave and came hurtling down the face of it into a full roll. As she righted herself, Dubois heard a deafening crash. The mast had crashed down onto the deck and was broken in three places. Part of the mast had broken a porthole and as the boat rolled about, water gushed into the cabin. Inside the boat, the contents of cupboards had been flung across the compartment and were floating in the water on the floor.

Dubois knew he had to cut part of the mast free so that it wouldn't do further damage if the boat was knocked down or rolled again. Amidst the chaos in the cabin he found a saw and a knife and scrambled out onto the deck. He knew if he attempted to stand he would be blown or swept overboard so he crawled to the broken mast. He managed to cut free the mast section and was relieved to see that he still had a stay sail and a boom. He reckoned that when the conditions eased he would be able to cobble together a makeshift rigging which would get him to the Australian coast.

Dubois began some repairs, confident that later he would be able to do more radical work. But the shrieking winds and big waves did not subside. A few hours later, after frequent knock downs the yacht rolled again, this time from the opposite side. Dubois was thrown against the side of the cabin and fell onto the floor. Once again, he pulled himself up and took stock of the situation. He had lost his ARGOS beacon, so he activated the second beacon and carried on with his repairs. It was Sunday evening and his signal was picked up at race headquarters in France. By this time Dubois was 1500 nautical miles south-west of Perth.

Just 13 nautical miles away from *Pour Amnesty International*, Tony Bullimore was having a cup of tea and a cigarette as he contemplated the storm. Earlier in the day he heard a radio report of a tropical storm off New Zealand with raging 70-knot winds. Throughout the day Bullimore had been monitoring the steady increase in the winds and hoping he was not heading into similar conditions. He had battened down and had been steering at the helm for about eight hours. He had considered attempting to steer right through the storm but, like Dubois, he eventually opted for the pilot and went below. With no sails up he was making about 20 knots and had to work hard to get the *Global Exide Challenger* at the best angle to the wind.

Wearing thermal underwear and oilskins over his clothes, Tony Bullimore was sitting comfortably in the galley, fairly relaxed, but prepared for anything. The yacht was holding up in the storm and Bullimore was pretty confident he could hold on that way until the storm blew itself out. Then, with no warning, he heard a very loud and distinct cracking noise and within seconds the yacht capsized, quietly and very quickly. Bullimore was amazed and confused, but unhurt. With characteristic calm, he lit another cigarette and took stock of the situation. His lead-ballasted keel had snapped and the boat stayed upside down in the water, pitching on the waves. Bullimore knew that the worst thing possible had happened, so he took plenty of time to consider what he should do next. Above the noise of the raging storm, he could hear a tapping outside as the foremast boom knocked against a window of the doghouse. In circumstances which would have sent many experienced sailors into a state of complete panic, Bullimore smoked his cigarette and made his plans in the darkness.

Thierry Dubois snatched some sleep and woke on Monday morning to unchanged weather conditions. As he lay in the comfort of his sleeping bag he felt the boat go slowly and smoothly into a roll. He was tipped out of his bunk and onto the underside of the deck. *Pour Amnesty International* was designed to be self-righting in accordance with the race's regulations, and Dubois waited for the yacht to swing back into an upright position. But it did not happen. The yacht was upside down, keel intact, and that was where she stayed.

Despite the mountainous seas, the yacht was quite stable and moved only with the swell. The portholes had split under the pressure and water was slowly leaking in. The flow increased as the water caused the openings to grow bigger. But Dubois had faith in the boat and the ocean itself. He was sure one of the huge waves which had knocked him down and rolled him over would knock him over again, this time into an upright position. He put on his survival suit and waited for his yacht to turn upright again.

But Dubois waited in vain. After two hours the boat had not moved and the roof was rapidly filling with water. It looked increasingly likely that *Pour Amnesty International* was going to stay upside down. Dubois considered setting off his beacon but wasn't sure about the efficacy of signalling from inside the hull of the boat. He decided to go out through the rear trap and prepare his life raft. He collected some safety gear and squeezed up through the hatch. Hanging onto the rope of the life raft, he clambered onto the upturned hull.

The yacht was rising and falling on the big waves and Dubois found it difficult to stay on the downward curve of the hull. He hung on tightly to one of the rudder blades as he switched on one of the beacons. As he turned his attention to the raft he saw that it had drifted several hundred metres away. Dubois was horrified. The raft contained all his emergency provisions and had been his one piece of security. Now there was nothing but the curving expanse of *Pour Amnesty International*'s upturned hull. Dubois clung to the rudder but was soon knocked off the hull by the force of a large wave, the first of many. He swam back to the boat and struggled up onto the hull. Dubois was over-whelmed by the hopelessness of the situation. Without food and water he knew he would not be able to survive for long, and the waves were constantly washing him into the terribly cold water. It could be hours, probably days, before he was found. There was nowhere else to go and nothing else he could do.

Tony Bullimore was worried about the boom tapping on the doghouse window but there was nothing he could do about it. The boat was still fairly dry inside and he put on his survival suit. He felt his best chance of rescue was if he stayed with the *Global Exide Challenger*, but he wanted to set up his life raft with all his gear, provisions and survival kit so that it would be ready if the situation deteriorated. He planned to inflate the life raft and tie it on a long rope so that it would not rub or knock against the hull and get ripped. To do this he would have to open the hatch and go out of the boat. As he opened the hatch it immediately slammed back down. The pain was sudden and excruciat-ing—the hatch had completely sliced off the top of his little finger. Bullimore quickly dunked it in the freezing water for about ten minutes to numb the pain.

The temperature was around zero and Bullimore was very cold. He was rethinking his plans when he heard another crash then a noise like a great waterfall. The boom that had been knocking against the doghouse window had smashed through and water was pouring in. Bullimore knew he had to find a dry space to try and keep warm. He settled on a small upturned shelf about half a metre wide and one and a quarter metres long. It was a tiny, cramped space and the space above gave him only about half a metre of head-room. Bullimore used some netting to fix a makeshift hammock which would stop him rolling off the shelf when the boat moved about. Having built his cubby he then set off his EPIRB. Soon after that he pushed one of the ARGOS beacons out through the cracked window. It seemed to float to the surface without getting caught in the rigging.

Bullimore was still determined to set up the life raft. Since the cabin window had broken, the *Global Exide Challenger* had taken on a lot more water. As he moved through the interior of the boat the water was as high as his chest, and in some areas it was easier to swim than walk. Bulli-more tried several times to free the raft but he realised it wasn't going to work. Even in its container the raft was buoyant and this was pinning it to the cockpit's sole. Even if he managed to free the raft it would be difficult for him to get it onto the surface of the water. Bullimore swam back to his cubby and tried to get warm as he considered his next move.

It was almost 1.00 a.m. on Monday, 6 January when signals from the ARGOS beacons on *Pour Amnesty Inter-national* and *Global Exide Challenger* were picked up in France. The alert was passed to the Rescue Coordination Centre in Canberra who alerted the RAAF and the navy. What followed was a mammoth and complex operation involving naval strategists, defence personnel and many civilians. It was vital that the rescuers and rescue equipment reached the yachts' location in the Southern Ocean as soon as possible. The location was approximately 1500 nautical miles north of Antarctica and the temperatures were somewhere between zero and five degrees Celsius. The strong winds were freezing and hypothermia would soon take a hold on the yachtsmen.

The rescue coordinators did not know whether Bullimore and Dubois were injured, still in their boats, in life rafts or in the ocean, and so they had to cater for every possible eventuality. The first task was to find the men. The job would have to be done from the air, and instructions were passed to the RAAF at Edinburgh Air Base, Adelaide, for an Orion P3 aircraft and crew to undertake the search. Flight Lieutenant Ludo Dierickx was at home fast asleep in bed when the decision was made that he would captain the Orion Rescue 251. His wake-up call was at 3.00 a.m. and just after 6.00 a.m. he was airborne with a 12-person crew and heading for the Southern Ocean via a refuelling stop in Perth.

Around the same time, the RAN guided missile frigate HMAS *Adelaide* with a Seahawk helicopter, was called upon to depart as soon as possible. If there were any survivors she would bring them back to shore. The HMAS *Adelaide* was based at HMAS Stirling, Western Australia. The frigate's skipper Captain Raydon Gates estimated that it would take until Thursday to cover the 1400 nautical miles to reach the yachtsmen. The question in the minds of the rescuers was whether the two men would be able to survive the freezing conditions for four days.

Thierry Dubois had lost count of the number of times he had been washed off the hull of *Pour Amnesty International* and into the freezing water. Each time he fought his way back to his position by the rudder and each time he was dashed against the hull. His head and face throbbed with pain from where the water had smashed his face against the rudder, his lips and nose taking the worst of the blow. He knew it would be a long time before he could expect any sign of rescue, and that every moment he remained perched on his upturned yacht was life threatening.

Dubois had considered trying to get back inside the boat but the hatch door had snapped shut. The boat had sunk lower in the water and there was no way he could get back inside. Apart from the hull, the only other place for him was in the water and he knew he would die there in a very short time. While the freezing winds and 12-metre waves lashed about him Dubois hung on grimly for his life. Suddenly, to his amazement, he saw an aircraft. Its arrival was hours earlier than he had anticipated and he thought it must be looking for someone else, perhaps Tony Bullimore, who had been the competitor closest to his own position.

Dubois felt a huge surge of relief. He knew that an actual rescue was still a long way off. A helicopter was needed to winch him off the hull and a ship was needed to bring the helicopter close enough to the area. He knew it would take a while for a ship to reach his position, but all the same, he was overjoyed. Here was life! He waved frantically to the aircraft crew. Just to have someone see him and know he was there was, at that moment, the most incredible and wonderful thing.

The Orion had arrived in the general area just before 4.00 p.m. To begin the search, Flight Lieutenant Dierickx had brought the aircraft down below the cloud cover to a height of about 100 metres. While state-of-the-art technology had brought them to the location at an incredible speed, it was the human eye which would find the men and their boats. The crew were scanning the churning water with intense concentration, fearing always that they might miss a small head bobbing above the water or mistake the white hull of a yacht for a surge of white water. The aircraft had only been in the area for 15 minutes when the crew spotted the upturned hull of *Pour Amnesty International*. Her keel was boldly standing up above the water and Thierry Dubois, a tiny figure in his red survival suit and bright yellow hood, was clutching the rudder. Dubois was waving to them and a cheer went up in the Orion. They had found their first man.

Dierickx had taken part in the search for Dinelli just a few days earlier, but the conditions he was experiencing that day were worse. He had to fly low in 60-knot winds so that a pair of rafts could be dropped upwind and hopefully straddle the boat. When they drifted down, Dubois would be able to grab the rope and pull himself onto one of the rafts. But the yacht's keel was acting like a sail and causing *Pour Amnesty International* to move faster than the rafts could drift. The joy Dubois felt when he saw the rafts drop soon evaporated when they were swept out of reach. The aircraft turned and attempted a second drop, but again the rafts landed some distance from the boat. Dubois was fairly certain that the aircraft would not make another attempt so in desperation he plunged into the water and swam towards the raft. To his enormous relief, he managed to grab the rope and haul himself aboard. The raft took off downwind at a great pace but he had only been aboard for a few minutes when he realised that the raft was damaged and was starting to sink. Frantically, he signalled to the Orion, but visibility in the aircraft was very poor. They passed over him, dropping a smoke signal, and left the area to look for the *Global Exide Challenger*.

Dubois' position was now worse than ever. He was a long way from his boat and his raft was sinking. A wave the size of a two-storey building loomed above him, then toppled the sinking raft and threw him back into the water. He rolled over under the raft, tangled in rubber and ropes. Gasping and spluttering, he managed to free himself and bob up to the surface of the water. He was alone again and it looked like the end. He had no choice but to battle the huge ocean and embark on a desperate swim back to his yacht. He struggled against the massive force of the water, every sinew straining to keep himself afloat and move towards the gleaming white hull and its tall keel. He had felt calm through it all, but now a sense of panic was sweep-ing over him. He kept on swimming, trying to close the distance between himself and the yacht. It was as though all feeling had left his body. His raft had gone, his boat was out of reach and the aircraft had left. He was grasping his last chance at life and he wondered how many minutes it would be before he would die, whether it would take long and what it would be like.

For a full half hour Dubois swam through the raging

ocean and reached his boat just as another Orion aircraft, Rescue 252, arrived at the scene. Rescue 252 was piloted by Flight Lieutenant Ian Whyte who only days before had led the search for Raphael Dinelli. Knowing he was just a tiny speck in the water, Dubois frantically waved a piece of orange fluoro he had kept from the damaged raft. The well-trained eyes of the Rescue 252 crew were expecting to see Dubois in the raft dropped by Rescue 251 but instead, caught sight of the bobbing yellow-hooded head and the waving orange rubber. Immediately they prepared to drop another life raft to him. Rescue 252 circled above the churning waves and came down as low as safety would permit. The task required split-second timing and absolute accuracy for the life raft to drift within Dubois's reach, and they succeeded. The drop was spot-on. Despite utter exhaustion, Dubois swam furiously in a last-ditch struggle to grab the raft ropes. He knew his survival so far was a miracle and this knowledge gave him the final burst of energy he needed to drag himself along the rope and into the raft. Thierry Dubois was in for a long, cold wait but at least he had some protection now. He had the life raft and a survival pack containing some food and water. Best of all he had the extraordinary gift of a second chance.

Pilot Ludo Dierickx and the crew of Rescue 251 had gone on to look for the *Global Exide Challenger*. They were running out of flying time and had to head for home, so they handed over the search to Rescue 252. About half an hour after Rescue 252 sighted Dubois, there was a whoop of delight in the aircraft as they spotted the hull of the *Global Exide Challenger*. It was about 9.30 p.m. on

Monday, 6 January. The curved white hull was pitching on the big waves but there was no sign of Tony Bullimore or his life raft.

The signals being picked up by satellite from the *Global Exide Challenger*'s ARGOS beacon had changed in such a way that it indicated human intervention. It seemed that Bullimore might still be alive and in the upturned hull of his boat. The operation took on another level of urgency. If Bullimore was still alive in the yacht it was essential to get to him as quickly as possible. He might be running out of air, as well as developing hypothermia. If he could not hear or see the search aircraft as Dubois had done, he might well lose hope, a vital factor in his survival.

Tony Bullimore was very much alive. When the yacht's keel had broken off it had left an open slot in the boat. So although the water level inside was rising, Bullimore was not short of air. He was very cold but still calm. Having given up any attempts to get the raft free he knew his only hope was to have faith in the ARGOS and EPIRB and wait for help to arrive. Most of his supplies had been swept out of the broken window of the doghouse as the water had rushed in. But in a frantic swoop, he had managed to capture some chocolate and some water. He knew he would have to wait at least three or four days before being rescued, so he rationed them carefully. He needed to conserve his energy to get himself through the long cold wait in the darkness.

Bullimore is a man of sturdy build and it was very uncomfortable in his tiny bolthole. But at least it was dry and in his perilous situation gave him some security. The hammock he had rigged up meant that even when the upturned boat rolled dramatically he would not fall out of his nest. He had one very wet, cold towel and he rolled and folded this into a pillow. He was thankful for his unusual ability to fall asleep anywhere, a skill he had perfected long ago. In the days to come Bullimore's ability to sleep enabled him not only to recharge his batteries, but also provided him with several hours of peaceful oblivion which helped pass the time.

Although the rescue services had located the *Global Exide Challenger* and thought there was a chance Bullimore was still alive, Bullimore himself had no idea whether or not he had been spotted. He was resigned to the idea of a very long wait and his determination, strength of character and knowledge of the sea allowed him to conserve his energy and keep his spirits up. When he was not sleeping he kept himself busy by moving around in the water inside the boat, making sure that things had not deteriorated further.

Bullimore could tell by the light filtering through the water whether it was day or night, but he had completely lost track of time and was no longer sure what day it was. It all seemed very much the same in the freezing, pitch dark cave of the overturned boat. His frequent attempts to set off more beacons and free the raft were painful, fruitless expeditions. He would dive into the freezing darkness of the water and struggle with the tangled ropes as his lungs strained to bursting point. Each time he returned to his shelf and hammock, unsuccessful and shaking with cold. He would huddle up in his bolthole, trying to get warm and build up energy so he could try again. The hours passed in a dark and lonely daze of cold, struggle, work and sleep.

Bullimore's greatest fear was that rescuers would come into the area, see the boat and not realise that he was inside it. He contemplated how he might be able to cut a hole in the hull so he would be able to set off a rocket if he heard the sound of rescuers outside. The noise of the wind and the thunder of the ocean drowned out almost all other sounds. He still felt his only chance of survival was to stay with the boat but his hope and confidence were running out. There was no more bottled water, but Bullimore did have a survival water maker which could convert the salt water to drinkable water. That, together with the remaining chocolate, kept him going.

A few nautical miles away, Thierry Dubois was also enduring his own cold and lonely wait in the raft. His isolation had been relieved a little when Rescue 253 had successfully dropped a radio to him. The radio in its red and white striped container was not designed to be dropped in an ocean location and there was only a one in a million chance of achieving a bullseye drop. The aircraft had descended to such a low level above the raft that its windows became encrusted with salt from the spray. But despite buffeting winds, the crew managed to get the radio onto the raft. The aircraft crew told Dubois that the HMAS *Adelaide* was on its way and that he could expect to be picked up late Wednesday or Thursday morning. He had some food and drink and this, together with his regular short chats with the aircraft crew, gave him strength.

Dubois' hardest battle was with the cold. At times he

feared he would freeze to death before the ship reached him. Water had got into his survival suit and he was frozen to the bone. He was particularly concerned about his feet which were so cold he could barely feel them. In the early stages of hypothermia the body draws warm blood from the extremities and the danger of frostbite was very real to Dubois. He remembered stories of alpine climbers whose feet froze and then they fell asleep and did not wake up. Unlike Bullimore, Dubois feared falling asleep. In order to stay awake, he would force himself to sponge or pump water out of the raft every half hour or so and sometimes he sang or shouted just to keep himself from drifting into sleep. He had also hurt his thumbs in one attempt to get onto the upturned keel and as they were extremely painful, he thought he might have broken them.

The days and nights seemed endless and Dubois was constantly amazed that he had not frozen to death or been overturned by the waves. When radio contact had been established, the Orion crew had told him that he could expect a slight improvement in the weather, and the conditions had certainly moderated. The aircraft crew had also told him that the Japanese tanker *Sanko Phoenix* was on her way and could possibly reach him before the HMAS *Adelaide*.

Bullimore and Dubois were not too far apart on the treacherous waters of the Southern Ocean, Bullimore in the tomb-like darkness of his yacht, and Dubois in the freezing cocoon of the life raft. But the comparatively short distance could do nothing to diminish their terrifying sense of isolation. Nor could it minimise the life-threatening conditions in which they passed their days and nights. As the aircraft crews circled and watched and the HMAS *Adelaide* made 26 knots towards them, they were still two human beings alone and on the knife's edge of survival in the most desolate ocean location on earth. While Dubois was reassured by the knowledge that rescue was on its way, Bullimore had no idea when, or if ever, rescuers would reach him.

Captain Raydon Gates of the HMAS *Adelaide* was considering his options. The weather forecast was grim and they could expect high seas, strong, icy winds and driving rain. The intention was for the Seahawk to fly to the *Global Exide Challenger*, winch the yachtsman into the helicopter and bring him to the safety of the ship. But the rescuers did not know what they would be facing when they reached the upturned yacht. Was Bullimore still alive inside the hull, and if so how were they to get him out? Would he be injured or would he be fit enough to help the rescuers' task? The option of sending divers to swim down under the boat was too hazardous as they could so easily become entangled in ropes or rigging. Gates was in contact with the skipper of the Japanese tanker which was due to arrive at the location around the same time as the HMAS *Adelaide*. One possibility was using the tanker's crane to lift the boat out of the water. Another option was cutting a hole in the hull of the *Global Exide Challenger* to enable Bullimore to get out on his own or to send a diver in to get him.

In the early hours of Wednesday, 8 January the rescue team received information from the designer of Bullimore's boat, which confirmed that it was possible he could still be alive beneath the hull. Some hours later, Rescue 256 dropped electronic equipment and sonobuoys into the ocean which would detect and relay sounds under the water's surface. The electronic noise equipment was picking up tapping noises in the *Global Exide Challenger* and the rhythm of the taps indicated that they were not mechanical, the sounds were being made by a human being. The crew of Rescue 256 were now sure that Tony Bullimore was still alive.

By mid-afternoon, the HMAS *Adelaide* was close enough to Dubois' location to contemplate rescuing him in the Seahawk. But the appalling weather conditions meant that, for the time being at least, the Frenchman would have to stay put. Raydon Gates had opted to cut a hole in the hull of the *Global Exide Challenger* and engineers, technicians and divers were busy working on the technical details. The winds and rain continued to rage across the ocean in the bleak darkness of the night. Dubois tossed in his freezing raft struggling to keep awake and Bullimore huddled in the pitch black bolthole of his yacht making vital drinking water.

At 7.30 a.m. on Thursday, 9 January, the weather had eased and the Seahawk, under the command of Lieutenant Commander Arthur Heather, took off from the HMAS *Adelaide's* deck and flew the 50 nautical miles to Dubois' raft. Back on board the frigate, Dr David Wright, the ship's doctor, was preparing the equipment and accommodation for two survivors. Rescue 260, with the same crew that had dropped the Frenchman his lifesaving raft, was in the air ready to guide the helicopter to Dubois' raft and coordinate the operation. In the left-hand seat was French Canadian Captain Mike Houde, with Ian Whyte as co-pilot. Although the winds had now dropped to 25 knots, flying below the clouds at about 90 metres was hazardous.

Thierry Dubois was overwhelmed by the moment. It seemed that the hours and days of waiting and hoping in the raft were at an end. He had been capsized in the boat, and later in the raft, and had swum for his life in the freezing and mountainous waters to get to this moment. Above him, he could see the Orion and the Seahawk breaking through the clouds above him. They were trying to locate him through the mist and rain and Dubois helped by using his radio to direct the helicopter downwind. Heather positioned the helicopter so a crewman could slowly be lowered to the raft. The air crews had explained the rescue procedure to him. He had gone over it again and again in his head, and now it was real. The crewman was slowly moving down, buffeted back and forth in the strong winds until he reached the raft. Dubois struggled into the rescue harness, feeling it clipped safely into place, then bid farewell to his cold wet cocoon of the past four days. As he was being winched up, he looked down on the sight which the air crews had seen so many times—the bobbing orange circle rocking on the great expanse of ocean.

Dubois scrambled into the belly of the helicopter. The deafening noise of the engines made conversation impossible, but he mouthed thanks to his rescuers and his beaming smile conveyed his huge gratitude and relief. A true professional, he carefully removed his gloves and hood and placed them in the appropriate sections of his survival suit before quietly reflecting on the rescue which, as he had floundered in massive seas only days before, had seemed impossible. As the Seahawk headed back to the HMAS *Adelaide*, it sent a message out, 'Tiger 74—we have a survivor on board, pigeons to mother,' and the crew of Rescue 260 cheered as they climbed to a higher altitude in order to seek out *Global Exide Challenger*.

Rescue 260 reached the location and stayed over the upturned yacht until the Seahawk arrived. The Orion was running out of flying time so once the helicopter arrived, it rose to 600 metres and returned to base. The helicopter was followed by the HMAS *Adelaide*. On board the frigate was the team of engineers and divers who would use a light-weight, rigid inflatable boat (RIB) to reach the upturned hull and cut a hole to free Bullimore.

Tony Bullimore was reviewing his life. It had not been a bad one and he had been lucky enough to do many of the things he wanted. In the dark and chilly corner of his yacht, he had grown accustomed to the noise of the ocean and the banging of the rigging against the hull these past four days. But as he lay there reflecting on his life, there seemed to be a different sort of banging. A stunning shiver of recognition swept over him. This was different! This banging was not some piece of the boat's equipment knocking with the motion of the sea. Bullimore struggled to his knees, his whole body on full alert. Straining to listen, he heard a human voice. Bullimore's voice burst from his throat and lungs. 'I'm coming! I'm coming out!' he yelled. The cry was charged with the intensity of his feelings—relief, excitement and the urgent need to get out of the boat.

Bullimore scrambled out of his bolthole. He plunged down into the dark water in the boat and swam frantically to the other end of the boat. Once out, he would not be able to go back—if he made a mistake it would all be over for him. But Bullimore was so sure of a human presence that he was prepared to take that risk. Gulping air into his lungs, he dived deep under the side of the boat and out of the cavernous darkness, his frozen limbs flailing to propel himself upwards to the surface. And there it was, the miracle he had dreamed of and longed for—men on the hull, others in an RIB, an aircraft overhead and further off the huge outline of the frigate. Tony Bullimore thought he was in heaven and barely noticed the cold of the water as he swam to the RIB. His rescuers, stunned by his sudden appearance in the water, quickly prepared to grab him and haul him to safety.

In the RIB, Chief Petty Officer Peter Wicker and Diver Alan Rub quickly wrapped Bullimore in foil blankets. Their joy and emotion at the sight of him was exceeded only by Bullimore's own euphoria. For this survivor there was no silent exhaustion. The words poured from his mouth as he struggled to thank his rescuers and see what was happening. His bare hands were frozen, his face bruised and he had a black eye but Bullimore was taking in everything he could. One frozen hand reached up to Wicker's face and he kissed the bearded sailor in his relief. Just minutes later, the RIB was alongside the HMAS *Adelaide* and Tony Bullimore was lifted to the warmth and safety of the frigate. Four hours earlier Thierry Dubois had set foot on the deck of the HMAS *Adelaide* and now the frigate had her second survivor. Tony Bullimore, on a stretcher, was on his way to join Thierry Dubois in the ship's sick bay. He was suffering from hypothermia, frost-bite, cuts and bruises and had lost the top of his little finger but hardly seemed aware of his injuries. Like Dubois he was relishing the ecstasy of being given a second chance at life.

On board the HMAS *Adelaide* the crew enjoyed the thrill and satisfaction of a highly professional operation carried out with 100 per cent success. They were part of a huge team which included the Orion crews, the shore-based defence personnel and civilians, the team at the Rescue Coordination Centre, and many more. Each individual had thrown their energy, experience, knowledge and their will into the fight to rescue the two yachtsmen from the jaws of death. They had all earned the laurels which soon began to flood in from around the world.

Within an hour Bullimore was on his feet and the two men faced the contingent of newspaper reporters who had travelled out with the HMAS *Adelaide*. Bullimore loqua-cious and ebullient, and Dubois thoughtful and stunned with gratitude, told their stories which were flashed around the world. Later they watched on video the scenes of their own delivery from the ocean. As the HMAS *Adelaide* made her way back to Fremantle, each man in his own characteristic way relived the experience and made the first steps back to physical and mental health. Bullimore went into a spin of activity, talking and walking around the ship until David Wright begged him to rest and get off his frostbitten feet. Dubois was more subdued and needed hyperbaric treatment to treat the frostbite on his feet and fingers. But they were alive and loving it.

The HMAS *Adelaide* arrived in Fremantle on Monday, 13 January and the eyes of the world watched as the two yachtsmen stepped onto Australian soil. A reception committee of local and national dignitaries, reporters from print and electronic media and thousands of West Australians who had turned out to welcome them, cheered the survivors and the heroic rescue crews. The rapturous cheers of the crowds and the hundreds of British and Australian flags waving on Fremantle's Victoria Quay was reminiscent of the welcomes staged for returned servicemen and women. The rescues were a triumph for Australia's defence forces and the civilian personnel who had set out to achieve the impossible and won. With outstanding courage, bravery and professionalism they had carried out the largest and most dramatic peacetime rescue in Australia's history.

Thierry Dubois' voice shook with emotion as he addressed the crowd. 'We are not the heroes,' he said. 'It's the seamen who have the spirit of help. Thank you to all these guys.' Tony Bullimore gestured to the rescuers who stood around him as he spoke of their professionalism, courage and dedication. Without them, he said, he would not have survived. 'If it wasn't for the defence forces and this great ship here, and every man and woman who sails on this ship, the professionalism and dedication, the inbuilt spirit of Australia, I'm positive, I'm absolutely no doubt at all positive I wouldn't be here now [sic]. I've been given another chance and it's through the efforts of Australia.'

Sources

Chapter 1

Drama off the West Australian Coast, Vic Jeffrey, The Royal Australian Navy, April 1985.

The *Daily News*, 14 and 15 February 1955.

The *West Australian*, 15, 16 and 17 February 1955.

The *Daily News*, 15 February 1955.

Chapter 2

The *Sydney Morning Herald*, 26–30 August 1969.

The *Courier Mail*, 26–30 August 1969.

The *Canberra Times*, 26–29 August 1969.

Report of the Court of Marine Enquiry, Melbourne. Under Section 364 of the Navigation Act 1912–1968: As to the Circumstances of the Foundering of the Motor Vessel *Noongah* off Nambucca Heads, New South Wales, 25 August 1969. Handed down, 16 February 1970.

Minutes of the Board of the Australian Coastal Shipping Commission, The Australian National Line, Meeting No. 150, 17 September 1969.

Australian Shipping Commission, 'The Australian National Line 1956–1981', R. Clark, L. Rex and D. Robertson, World Ship Society, Kendal, England 1982.

Australian Shipping Commission Annual Report, 1970.

Chapter 3

The *Courier Mail*, 4–13 October 1971.

The *Sun Herald*, 10 October 1971.

The *Sydney Morning Herald*, 4–13 October 1971.

The *Australian*, 8, 9 October 1971.

The *Sunday Australian*, 10 October 1971.

The *Daily Mirror*, 11–15 October 1971.

Author interview with Peter Dabbs, May 1997.

Author interview with Commander Terry Roach, May 1997.

Chapter 4

The *Courier Mail*, 10 May 1989.

The *Sunday Mail*, 11 May 1989.

'Miracle on the North East Passage' Peter Webster, *Australian Boating*, June 1989.

'Where Are They Now', television series, Channel 7, 15 March 1997

Author interview with Colin Ward, 1 May 1997.

Chapter 5

The *Sunday Times*, 25 March 1984.

Daily News, 24 March 1984.

The *Courier Mail*, 24, 25, 26 March 1984.

The *West Australian*, 26 March 1984.

The *Northern Territory News*, 23 March 1984.

Australia's Northern Prawn Fishery; The first 25 years, Peter C. Pownall (ed), NPF25, Cleveland Australia, 1994.

Big Blow Up North, Kevin Murphy, University Planning Department, Darwin, 1994.

Author interview with Richard Samuels, April 1997.

Author interview with Chris Terjesen, May 1997.

Author interview with Reg Brown, May 1997.

Chapter 6
The *Daily Telegraph*, 27 April 1989.
The *Sydney Morning Herald*, 27 April 1989.
The *Australian*, 27 April 1989.
Australia Sea Safety Awards Bulletin (undated).
Author interview with Lyn and Bryce Quarrie, 28 April
    1997.

Chapter 7
The *Courier Mail*, 10 March 1990.
Gold Coast Bulletin, 10, 15 March 1990, 23 January 1993.
Queensland Police Vedette, October 1990.
Gold Coaster, 10 March 1990.
Radio Log of Calls from Gold Coast Water Police, 8, 9
    March 1990.
Situation Report and Final Summary EPIRB Catamaran
    Moana Ari, Sea Safety Centre, Canberra, 9 March 1990.
Search and Rescue of Two Persons from Catamaran *Moana
    Ari*, Gold Coast District Water Police Report, Sergeant
    s/c Peter Stiller, reprinted in *Multihull Magazine*, June
    1990.
Author interview with Constable Kyle Bates, 7 May 1997.
Author interview with Julian Martin, May 1997.

Chapter 8
Gold Coast Bulletin, 3 October 1990.
The *Courier Mail*, 3 October 1990.
'Ascent to Terror', Tracey Aubin, Readers Digest, Australia,
    March 1991.
Author interview with Roger Meadmore, 10 May 1997.

Chapter 9

Departmental Investigation into the Loss of the Bow Section of the Greek Registered Motor Tanker *Kirki*—the Subsequent Fire, Evacuations of the Crew and Salvage Operation From 20 July 1991 to 23 August 1991, Report 33, Department of Transport and Communications.

MT *Kirki* Oil Pollution Incident Report, Department of Marine and Harbours, Western Australia, Australian Maritime Safety Authority, BP, Esso, AIP.

United Salvage *Kirki* (Video) United Salvage Pty Ltd and Silver Wing Films Pty Ltd.

The *West Australian*, 22, 23, 24, 25 July 1991.

The *Australian*, 22, 23, 24 July 1991.

The *Sunday Times*, 28 July 1997.

The *Log of the Western Gateway*, Monthly Bulletin of the WA Branch of the Company of Master Mariners, August 1991.

Chapter 10

The *Australian*, 29–31 December 1994, 1–3 January 1995.

The *Adelaide Advertiser*, 29–31 December 1994, 1, 2, 4 January 1995.

The *Sydney Morning Herald* 1–4 January 1995.

The *Sunday Times* (WA) 1 January 1995.

The *West Australian* 30, 31 December 1994, 2, 3 January 1995.

Yachting—the Official Magazine of the BOC, vol. 176, Issue 7, Jan 95; vol. 176, Issue 8, Feb 95; vol. 176, Issue 9, Mar 95; http://stono.cs.cofc.edu.boc/info/arts/yacht5.html

The Unofficial BOC Home Page Race Reports, http://
stono.cs.cofc.ed. . .reports

Chapter 11
The *Sydney Morning Herald*, 27, 28 December 1996,
4 January 1997.
The *Weekend Australian*, 11, 12 January 1997.
The *West Australian*, 28 December 1996.
The *Australian*, 9 January 1997.
The *Bulletin*, 21 January 1997.
'I Was His Only Hope', by Peter Goss, *Yachting World*,
March 1997.
'All I Could Do Was Wait', by Raphael Dinelli, *Yachting
World*, March 1997.
The *Vendee Globe Newsletter*, 29 May 1996, http://
www.vendee-globe. . .ge/newsletter290596.html
Rescue in the Southern Ocean, coordinators Martin Daly
and Sally Dugon of the *Age*, Penguin Books, Australia
1997.
ABC Television News, 27, 28 December 1997.

Chapter 12
ABC Television News, 4–13 January 1997.
Southern Ocean Survival, Quantum, ABC Television,
March 1997.
The *Australian*, 7–10 & 13–15 January 1997.
The *Weekend Australian*, 11, 12 January 1997.
The *Sydney Morning Herald*, 7–10 January 1997.
The *Age*, 7–10, 13, 15 January 1997.
The *Sunday Times*, 12 January 1997.

The *West Australian*, 7–10 & 13–15 January 1997.

The *Bulletin*, 21 January 1997.

Info Vendee Globe 96/97 Latitudes *Pour Amnesty International*, Thierry Dubois Reaccent, http://www.in-net.fr/latitudes/Th Dubois.html

Defence News Releases, Defence Public Relations, 6 January 1997, March 1997

The *Vendee Globe Newsletter*, 29 May 1996, http://www.vendee-globe. . .ge/newsletter290596.html

'Full Tilt Test', Dan Dickinson, *Sailing World*, December 1996.

Vendee Globe Solo-non-stop-around-the-world Race Summary & French assessment at mid point of race by Philippe Jeantot, Texas Sailing News, http://www.sailtexas.com/vendee.html

'Drama in the Southern Ocean', *Yachting World*, March 1997.

'Tony Bullimore—The Inside Story', *Yachting World*, March 1997.

Rescue in the Southern Ocean, coordinators Martin Daly and Sally Dugon of the *Age*, Penguin Books, Australia 1997.

Picture Credits

1, 2 – The *West Australian*

3 – George Lipman, The Fairfax Photo Library

4, 5 – Courtesy of Mr Terry Roach and the RAN

6, 7, 8, 9, 10, 11 – John Heselwood, Channel 7 Brisbane

12 – Courtesy of Kailis Fisheries, Perth

13 – The *Courier Mail*, Brisbane

14, 15 – Courtesy of Lyn and Bryce Quarrie

16, 17 – Channel 9, Brisbane

18, 19 – Courtesy of Neil Eliot, The *Australian*

20, 22, 23 – Courtesy of the RAAF

21 – Nicholas Wilson, The *Advertiser*, Adelaide

24 – Kerry Berrington, The *Sunday Times*, Perth

25 – Guy Magowan, The *West Australian*